. . . AND EVERY DAY YOU TAKE ANOTHER BITE

LARRY MERCHANT

A DELL BOOK

FOR HEIDI

Published by
DELL PUBLISHING CO., INC.
750 Third Avenue
New York, New York 10017
Copyright © 1971 by Larry Merchant
All rights reserved. For information, address
Doubleday & Company, Inc.

Dell ® TM 681510, Dell Publishing Co., Inc.
Reprinted by arrangement with
Doubleday & Company, Inc.
New York, New York 10017
Printed in the United States of America
First Dell printing—October 1972

CONTENTS

1. Colts XVI, Cowboys XIII   9
2. Political Football   29
3. Snake Oil and Profundity   67
4. Men Attend, Women Comprehend   87
5. N. Tangibles and Mo Mentum   109
6. St. Vince   135
7. The Sensuous Quarterback   153
8. Tale of Two Cities   175
9. Clear but Loud   211
10. Fugue for Grid Horns   229
    STOP ACTION   245

1. COLTS XVI, COWBOYS XIII

David was asked to explain how the out-manned Israelites beat the first-place Philistines.

"Our game plan," David said, "was the old-fashioned strategy of breaking down the opposition at its strongest point. So I went one-on-one with Goliath."

"Wasn't that dangerous? He's listed in the Philistine press guide as 6-8 and 270 pounds and he made All-Asia Minor three straight years."

"As my high school coach used to say, it's not the size of the man, it's the size of the heart in the man. I have to give credit to our scouts too. They told us Goliath used a zone defense and liked to rotate to the weak side. I just slingshot into the seams. And the line, don't forget the line. I got great protection."

"Didn't you put yourself on the spot earlier in the week?"

"I guaranteed it," David said with a grin, "because I knew we had God on our side."

"You mean . . ."

"We're No. 1."

THE scenario of the 1971 Super Bowl was written with a pen dipped in slapstick irreverence. It was written by someone who thinks that football is a terrific game and a colorful spectacle and—you won't believe this, sports fans—no more, no less. Someone who sees the rest of the pro football mystique, from the cosmic musings of deep thinkers to the patriotic posturing of shallow thinkers to the huckstering Barnum of double thinkers, as a perfect spiral of lunacy.

The National Football League, according to this scenario, promoted the 1971 Super Bowl as SUPER BOWL V, so we could swoon at its self-image of epic grandeur. Presumably the Roman numeral was affixed to our gladiatorial circus to honor Proconsul Pete Rozelle and St. Vince Lombardi. Or to make certain we understood the gravity and significance of the event. Some of us had mistaken it for a mere game but Kenneth Clark surely would turn it into a chapter of *Civilisation,* his history of art. Unlike the World Series, which is simply the World Series, and the Kentucky Derby and the U. S. Open and the Indianapolis 500, this was SUPER BOWL V. A roll of drums and a flourish of trumpets, please.

The Baltimore Colts then beat the Dallas Cowboys XVI to XIII on a field goal with V seconds to play. But the game was something less than art or history. Many observers thought it was something less than football, at least as the professionals are supposed to play it. Whatever it was, it was entertaining, and instructive. It featured a total of XI fumbles and interceptions and XIV penalties (for MLXIV yards) .

Depending on where you sat, or on whom you bet, this was either sacrilege or side-splitting comedy. One vote for comedy. It was a whipped-cream pie in the face of the pretentious boobs dedicated to making the NFL an eternal flame of truth, the quintessence of America. It was a banana peel under the anointed memory of Vince Lombardi, who was officially canonized for the occasion. It was a pair of baggy pants on television, which viewed the thing as though it were a solemn high mass.

The starting line-ups should have provided the first clue of what the day would bring:

BALTIMORE	POS.	DALLAS
Groucho Marx	WR	Bert Lahr
Woody Allen	WR	Jerry Lewis
Danny Kaye	TE	W. C. Fields
Stan Laurel	RT	Bob Hope
Jackie Gleason	RG	Jack Benny
Emmett Kelly	C	Pigmeat Markham
Jack E. Leonard	LG	Don Rickles
Buddy Hackett	LT	Godfrey Cambridge
Harpo Marx	QB	Craig Morton
Flip Wilson	RB	Harry Ritz
Phil Foster	RB	Bill Cosby

This should have immediately brought into question some of the unquestioned premises of the game. Controlled violence, they call it. A microcosm of our society, with its machine precision and organization men and plastic armor and film studies and psychologic probing and computer planning and sophisticated specialization. "A Game for Our Times," with millions of man-hours invested in recruiting talent, talent brimming with character and courage and pride and high moral purpose. With coaches of such Himalayan intellect that only their love of the game keeps them from becoming captains of industry or statesmen.

But once the Cowboys and the Colts managed to tie their shoelaces, with some difficulty, they seemed stumped. So they played it for laughs. And they were super.

It is no more possible to detail every master stroke of buffoonery than it would be to eat all the pigskin in Iowa. A few highlights will do.

I—The Cowboys recovered a fumble on the Colt 9-yard line but had to settle for a field goal. II—After Craig Morton completed what would be his lone completion to an end, Bob Hayes, the Cowboys were on the Colt 6-yard line and had to settle for another field goal. III—The Colts tied the score when Johnny Unitas overthrew a receiver and wound up with a touchdown when another receiver, John Mackey, caught the ball after a Cowboy or two tipped it—followed by a missed extra point. IV—The Cowboys went ahead 13—6 after recovering another fumble and driving 28 yards—the longest successful drive of the game. V—The half ended with the Colts frustrated on the Cowboy 2-yard line after by-passing a field-goal attempt. Alex Karras, the clown prince of the Detroit Lions, was heard to speculate that the Colts just might decide to pass up a second extra point if they got a second touchdown.

Both teams put on their size-18 shoes and grease paint for the second act. VI and VII—The Colts fumbled the kickoff but the Cowboys fumbled back to them near the goal line. VIII—Earl Morrall, who had replaced the injured Unitas late in the second quarter, completed a substantial pass-run play to a back whom the Cowboys neglected to cover; but then on third down Morrall, under pressure, ballooned the ball into the end zone instead of grounding it to keep the Colts in field goal range, and it was intercepted. IX—Moments later the Colts struck hilariously again. On a play designed for the quarterback to hand off to a halfback who laterals back to the quarterback who throws downfield—the same razzmatazz that Morrall mucked up against the Jets in the 1969 Super Bowl when he didn't see a man all alone—the halfback had to throw instead because the Cowboys wrapped up the quarterback. Eddie Hinton caught the ball and zipped toward the end zone, only to fumble when he was hit two strides away, whereupon the Cowboys took one Ritz Brother pratfall after another chasing and squibbing the loose ball until it slid out of the end zone for a touchback.

By this time the bald-headed guys in the front rows were yelling "Bring on the girls." They got Morton, and he outdid himself. He threw three interceptions in eight minutes. X—One set up the tying score. XI—One set up the winning score after the Cowboys had possession in Colt territory with less than two minutes left. XII—The third was a last-play desperation heave, and it brought down the house.

Jim O'Brien, the rookie who missed the extra point, kicked the field goal from the 32, touching off wild celebrations across the land. Not only did it win the game but it ended it. For 80,000 people in the Orange Bowl in Miami and for 60 million in televisionland, all on the edge of their seats anxious to see who would trip over what yard line next, it was a sublime climax. The threat of a lingering sudden-death playoff was extinguished. The danger of milking the gag beyond endurance was averted.

Now it isn't unusual for a football to take funny bounces: it is deliberately shaped the way it is to confound and deflate us. It especially isn't unusual when defensive-oriented teams meet because it is their purpose in life to make offensive teams nervous wrecks as well as physical wrecks. The Colts and Cowboys simply brought this collision of resistible forces and immovable objects to its logical conclusion, and further, to caricature.

ITEM: It is a rule of thumb that when a team coughs up the ball four times in a game it must lose, unless the other team catches the cough. Midway through the fourth quarter the Colts led in turnovers seven to one but the Cowboys led by only one touchdown. You think that's easy, try it some day. Better still, have your local high school team try it. Without ten coaches who have access to banks of computers, it will take a lot of practice.

ITEM: It is an article of faith among the faithful that quarterbacking is the name of the game (when third down, defense, hitting, emotion or something else isn't the name of the game). The quarterbacking in Super Bowl V was not even the middle initial. Except for his freak touchdown pass through what a clairvoyant sign labeled "The Friendly Skies of Unitas," Johnny Unitas, age thirty-seven, once great, was impotent. Earl Morrall, who had been exposed on the same field two years before, wasn't much better; he moved the Colts into scoring range three times and couldn't move them the rest of the way, which, after all, is the idea. It would be kicking a dead Cowboy to reflect on Craig Morton in gorier detail.

ITEM: The quarterbacks had gifted straight men. Other players with character, courage, pride, high moral purpose, et al., went to pieces in the big one. Bob Vogel, star offensive tackle for the Colts, admitted that he kept forgetting the snap count. Jocks are always blaming occult forces for variances in performance. What poor dumb vibration in the solar system got the blame this time?

ITEM: The coaches, as the earthly agents of God and the computers, had some curious moments too. Don McCafferty of the Colts made the XIIIth turnover when he decided to go for the touchdown instead of that field goal. Tom Landry, who called all the plays for Morton until the last two minutes, added to the merriment. Lulled by a precarious lead, he stuck to his game plan with the inflexibility of Buster Keaton's jaw despite the fact that it wasn't working. And he committed the last venal sin when he didn't use his time-outs as the Colts maneuvered into position for the winning field goal; he could have saved forty seconds for one final boffo fling.

But the game is far from the only thing on Super Sunday. This is pro football's showcase and they try to do it all. The showcase is a prism through which the holy and holier-than attitudes of the mystique, mixed in with the natural glories of football, are refracted in brilliant living color and deadly serious pretense.

The pre-game and half-time shows were typical medleys of tooting and bonging and flag waving. Before the game a formation of four jet fighter planes zoomed over the stadium, one of them peeling off, we were told, to symbolize the nation's concern for prisoners of war in North Vietnam. The planes arrived a couple minutes late but considering what went on in the game it was amazing that the symbolism didn't go down in flames. Similar flights of fantasy had taken place throughout the NFL for the last month of the season, following an attempt to rescue prisoners that its planners described as a heroic success although it failed in one minor detail: it rescued no prisoners. There was a much clearer relationship in that symbolism to the follies on the field.

At half time a lady who fancies herself the Voice of America, Anita Bryant, sang "The Battle Hymn of the Republic," also contributing to the fun and gaiety of the spectacle. An appearance by the University of Chicago marching band—fifty students roaming chaotically and kazooing kazoos—would have been more in tune with the game.

Fulfilling its role as copromoter with the NFL, television trained an unblinking but embarrassed battery of eyes on the show. The camera crews followed the bouncing ball faithfully, providing a continuous laugh-in of replays. But the announcers had difficulty with their focus. Not once did they indicate that something nutty was going on down there, that it wasn't classic playbook football but that it sure was an exciting mess, like a souffle that blows up in Graham Kerr's face. They reacted as though they were watching a squadron of Communist pigeons defiling the Tomb of the Unknown Soldier. They daren't, or didn't have the wit, to put the show into the bemused perspective it needed. Merchandising right down to the solemn signoff, Curt Gowdy gave a soap-opera tribute to Earl Morrall for avenging 1969.

With its genius for stretching time, television created a five-hour spectacular for the three-hour game. An hour eulogy to Vince Lombardi, oddly, was not accompanied by organ music. In football's version of *Love Story,* an interesting man of many dimensions was reduced to a cardboard-thin myth. The next half hour juxtaposed Joe Namath, the *enfant* outrageous who had succeeded Lombardi as the dominant figure in the game even before his death. Namath, in previewing the Colts and Cowboys, omitted the crucial possibility that the Cowboy rush might discombobulate Unitas. And he made excuses for Morton's allegedly injured arm (Morton having passed for five touchdowns in the last game of the regular season when the opposition was weak Houston). But, in the manner of the child who adds incorrectly but instinctively or accidentally comes up with the right sum, Namath picked the Colts to win. That, as they say, can't be coached. You've got it or you don't.

The post-game show offered the standard package of unasked and unanswered questions, and a weepy presentation ceremony. Mrs. Marie Lombardi gave a trophy named for her late husband to Carroll Rosenbloom, owner of the Colts. Her tears undoubtedly were inspired by the certain knowledge that the great coach in the sky would be raging like Jehovah over the sloppy exhibition and demanding that both teams report to practice Monday. Rosenbloom, as is the custom with athletes who suggest that somebody up there likes them best, muttered that it couldn't have been done without divine assistance. Nobody had put Craig Morton in that league before.

What was America thinking about all this? A market-research team of one found that many fans, their brains washed and bleached by the NFL mystique, felt betrayed by the inelegant play. Some fans were amused, others confused, but most ultimately were swept up by the theatrics. All but 231 of the viewers were emotionally spent—the 231 who hadn't bet on the game. Having sweated out their bets until the end (the Colts beat the spread by a half point), the remaining millions empathized with Rosenbloom's ashen looks and choked-up speech.

The research team found something else. Within this vast constituency there was a relevant political cleavage, polarized by Vietnam and President Nixon's identification with football. For the hard-nosed hawks who saw football as the last frontier of discipline, the red-white-and-blue pageantry was offset by the disorder of the game. For the soft-nosed doves who equated football with violence and jingoism, the slapstick should have been consolation for any indignities of propaganda socked to them. Both parties would have been wise to remember that nearly 150 million Americans chose to ignore the whole thing.

Thus another Super Bowl with a moral. In Super Bowl I the Green Bay Packers beat the Kansas City Chiefs XXXV to X, preserving the known laws of the universe, i.e., the superiority of the establishment. In Super Bowl II the Packers beat the Oakland Raiders XXXIII to XIV, reaffirming the omnipotence of Vince Lombardi. In Super

Bowl III Joe Namath and the New Yorks Jets beat the Colts XVI to VII, upsetting the known laws of the universe with a victory for impetuous youth. In Super Bowl IV the Chiefs beat the Minnesota Vikings XXIII to VII, confirming the new order. Later, in Super Bowl VI, the Cowboys beat the Miami Dolphins XXIV to III, with such deadly efficiency that many people looked back fondly to that time when they were lovable stumble-heroes.

The 1971 Super Bowl reminded us that pro football is a terrific game, not an exercise in technology or any other ology. And that there are powerful opportunists getting in the way of the game, exploiting it with their political and moral righteousness.

In a postscript, the scenario also reminded us, with the private misery of public men, that football is played by a large but not larger-than-life breed of homo sap. Lance Rentzel of the Cowboys, arrested a month earlier on charges of indecent exposure (to which he later pleaded guilty), didn't play. Johnny Unitas, it was revealed two days after the game, had been sued for divorce on the grounds of adultery.

As the NFL is fond of saying, any of this could happen on any given Sunday.

Let's take a look at that again on the instant isolated slow-mo replay . . . There's Snoopy in the
pocket, good protection, plenty of time, the classic
delivery . . .

Now here's Woodstock, the flashy little flanker who led the league in receiving last season. Looks like he's running a zig-in corner post flag slant up pattern . . .

All right, let's see what happened now. Woodstock had five yards on the cornerback, when, well, it looks like he tripped in the tall grass. Or maybe it was interference . . .

We'll wait for the call from the official on that. Back up field, Snoopy has a strange look of disgust on his face. You can't throw the ball much better than that . . .

2. POLITICAL FOOTBALL

Former President Lyndon Johnson, in a rare interview, said today that he made his biggest political blunder when he refused to take a foreign dignitary to a football game because he felt it showed the violent side of America.

Most observers believe that it cost him a second term in the White House.

The incident occurred in 1967. Protests poured in from his native state of Texas, where football is king, and sports columnists all over the country castigated the President. "But that's not what did it," Johnson said. "The extremists. The football fanatics. They wouldn't let go of it. They ran Eugene McCarthy, a former football player, against me in New Hampshire. Then that pep rally in Chicago. It was damn near a riot. I didn't have a chance."

The Republicans attached Johnson's anti-football stance to the entire Democratic Party, and it stuck despite the fact that the party rejected him. Johnson noted that President Nixon ran on a platform of a pro franchise in every city.

The leaders of the movement to oust Johnson, the famed Chicago Seven, are going to be installed in the Hall of Fame this year, alongside the immortal Seven Blocks of Granite of Fordham and Seven Mules of Notre Dame.

WHEREVER the President of the United States goes a man with a black satchel goes with him. This man is called "the man with the football." He is not the man, unfortunately, whose job it is to bring forth a football should the President be seized by an uncontrollable urge to frolic on the White House lawn. (Unlike the Kennedys, who were activists, President Nixon prefers the role of superfan; this rational approach to exercise, including the razing of the White House pool, has left him in apparent excellent health.) The black satchel is said to contain a series of codes that could be used to release our hydrogen bombs. Which is enough to make anyone start calling a long pass a plain old long pass again.

Stuff like that has given football a bad name in some places. Political football has evolved from a shopworn phrase to a disquieting attempt to take over the game by politicians and superpatriots. That is, the right wing is replacing the single wing and the double wing. There's no need to get hysterical over this, however, because, like the single wing and the double wing, and even the shotgun formation, the right wing's influence too shall pass. The rest of us football degenerates must think cool thoughts and dig the game for what it is, a game.

With President Nixon's blessing, strong-side-right fans have tried to capture football, as they periodically try to capture the flag. Their message to strong-side-left fans is clear: football, love it or leave it. Happily this won't be necessary. Superpatriotic pageantry and lofty harangues on the All-American virtues of the game are such a mindless bore that inevitably they'll backfire. When players begin to giggle during pre-game sermons and fanatics begin to wish they could retreat to a dressing room at the half, sanity is about to make a comeback.

Lyndon Johnson actually was the first President to admit to attending a professional game, an exhibition in Washington. The Redskins lost and afterward coach Otto Graham cracked that if that was all the President could do for his beleaguered team he might as well stay away. Both Johnson and Graham, coincidentally or not, were turned out of office after the season.

Until Richard Nixon made the team in Washington, as Vice-President and President, political football was merely an apt metaphor, no doubt related to the ancient definition of a pigskin as an agitated bag of wind. Politicians out of favor are

Center Play

viewed, usually by political cartoonists, as footballs being kicked around. Nixon himself, in a famous remark to reporters after he was defeated in a gubernatorial election in California in 1962, said they wouldn't have him to kick around anymore. But like those hoary old pros who go into one retirement after another when they suspect that their services may no longer be required, Nixon returned, and he returned triumphantly, as No. 1.

As if by executive fiat then, a second football term infiltrated, or blitzed, the language: game plan. The President's game plan for the Mideast was this, his game plan for the economy was that, his game plan for his next game plan was some other thing.

Senator Eugene McCarthy of Minnesota had a few words about that. It was McCarthy who elevated all sports metaphors to poetic heights in the presidential primaries of 1968. Among them: "Politics is like coaching football. You have to be smart enough to understand the game and dumb enough to think it's important." One of the President's game plans reminded him of a favorite play in college—"the forward fumble." When a nominee for the Supreme Court, Clement Haynsworth, was rejected by the Senate, Nixon grumbled that the South was a victim of prejudice. On the theory that he was making yardage with his southern fans after screwing up, McCarthy gave him a first down, if not a touchdown, for recovering the forward fumble.

Nevertheless the use and abuse of "game plan," through semantic overkill, has made an important point. For, as fans have come to know, a game plan is hardly a foolproof stratagem. The best laid game plans of coaches and presidents oft go awry. Senator Edmund Muskie, leading contender for the Democratic presidential nomination in 1972, took notice of that when he said, "We need more than a new game plan. We need a new coach." Vice-President Agnew responded with this: "I doubt seriously if Muskie's two yards and a cloud of dust is sufficient to impress even his fellow Democrats." Whoever wins the election, it's likely that we will get kicked groggy from goal line to goal line by such deadly dialogue.

President Nixon's involvement with football extends innocently from his roots as a third-string tackle at Whittier College to a not-so-innocent sense of public relations as politician. Pat Summerall, a television announcer, has recalled with astonishment how Vice-President Nixon once visited the locker room of the New York Giants and knew the players by their first names; television announcers are easily astonished. At a banquet for legendary jocks of yesteryear, with blowhards blowing hard on what the game does for America (much as butchers and hairdressers do about their game at such affairs), Nixon delivered a casual and winning remembrance of heroes past, like any fan thrilled to be in such company. Six points for that. And he obviously is no further away from yesterday's sports news than today's newspaper. After the 1971 Super Bowl he hoped aloud that he wouldn't make as many mistakes as the Colts and Cowboys had. When George Allen made a multiplayer trade at the college draft meeting ten days later, Nixon wired the new Redskin coach that he was looking forward to a championship in a year or two.

When the Redskins won their first five games of last season, the President reflected the local euphoria by playing Superfan. He sent Henry Kissinger on secret missions to peace conferences in Paris under the code name "quarterback." Peter Lisagor of the *Chicago Daily News* filed this report after a critical meeting with French President Pompidou:

> White House sources say frankly that the decision to agree on devaluation of the dollar was not made until the final meeting between the two Presidents and the best guess yesterday morning was that no agreement would be reached. This appears to have been confirmed by an unscheduled activity on Mr. Nixon's part. He stayed awake until 4:30 a.m. Azores time to listen to a radio broadcast of the Redskins—Los Angeles Rams football game. Twice he called Secretary of State Rogers to exult over Redskin touchdowns

and at the end of the game he woke his assistant, R. H. (Bob) Haldeman, to tell him the Redskins had won.

Back in Washington the President turned up at practice one day and asked the Redskins to run one of his favorite plays, a screen pass. Giddy with power, he recommended an end-around for a playoff game: the Redskins ran it—and lost 13 yards. Showing true grit, he then called Miami coach Don Shula at 1:30 a.m. to recommend a slant-in pass to Paul Warfield for the Super Bowl. "When the phone rang at that hour," said Shula, "I thought it might be some nut calling." Miami tried the standard play twice, unsuccessfully.

The players restrained themselves from reversing their roles and recommending new foreign policies, but Larry Csonka of Miami said in *Sport* magazine:

> The man upsets me with his role as a super-jock. Here he is, the one man in the world who has, at his fingertips, all the information and the influence to make a lot of peoples' lives better. But what's he doing calling football players on the telephone and giving pep talks to teams? He isn't going to help anybody. It just brainwashes people more, makes them think football is a lot more important to them than it really is. He's either hung up on violence, or else he's pulling off

a master con job on a lot of sports fans, he's implying that he's one of them and he's hoping to get their votes in return. Nixon may identify with football players, but I don't identify with him, and I haven't met a player yet who does.

The President's post-game telephone calls to victors can be seen as a harmless indulgence in hero worship and jock sniffing. His supporters might even claim they are acts of heroism themselves because for every Darrell Royal (Texas football coach) or Len Dawson (Kansas City quarterback) he can congratulate, there are a dozen uncalled victors he can alienate. After the New York Knickerbockers won the National Basketball Association championship in 1970 a prankster got through to Willis Reed in the dressing room by saying he was the President. Reed put the phone to his ear, realized he had been taken, huffed, "Higgledy-piggledy poop, Mr. President," and hung up. Reed's inspirational play, with a leg injury, certainly merited a presidential citation but his opponent, Wilt Chamberlain, was an active Nixonite.

Whatever his motive, Nixon also got tangled in a political thicket when he took it upon himself to declare unbeaten Texas the top college team in the country after a victory over Arkansas in 1969. Cynics were sure it was part of a bigger game plan to convert Texas to the Republican

'PENALTY? BUT WE'VE ONLY BEEN IN A HUDDLE 2 YEARS!

column in 1972. But there were angry repercussions in Pennsylvania, which already was Republican and was justly proud of equally unbeaten Penn State. The result could be a net loss of one electoral vote. It is unlikely that a belated (two months after the end of the season) telegram of congratulations, sent by Nixon to Kings College of Pennsylvania for being named the top club team of 1970, will undo the damage.

Meanwhile the Democrats were fighting back. Suddenly Lyndon Johnson, in retirement, was a highly visible presence at Texas games. Some observers interpreted this as a signal that he was hankering to get back into the big game in 1972. After Texas beat Notre Dame in the 1970 Cotton Bowl, Darrell Royal got a call from Nixon and a personal visit from Johnson in his dressing room. "Mr. President," yelped Royal, who was undressing when he opened the door, "you caught me with my long underwear showing."

Nixon watchers sniffed an escalation of political intrigue after the 1971 Cotton Bowl, when Notre Dame beat Texas. Curiously the President ignored the opportunity to make a pitch for the Catholic vote. Was it because of the Texas-Pennsylvania precedent? Or because the Reverend Theodore Hesburgh, chancellor of Notre Dame, had been critical of his administration? Or because Nebraska had emerged as the top team? Nixon made no definitive judgment but he did choose the Nebraska campus to deliver a speech on the youth of

America. The real importance of that speech was that it reassured football fans of his commitment to excellence. It was Nebraska Senator Roman Hruska, in defense of Harold Carswell, a second Supreme Court nominee rejected by the Senate, who made a historic gaffe when he said mediocre folks should have representation too.

No great truth can be gleaned from the Nebraska-Notre Dame episode, besides the added evidence that politicans have a pathological need to be associated with winners. Bobby Kennedy, as attorney general, removed an autographed photo of heavyweight champion Floyd Patterson from his office after Sonny Liston knocked him out.

The comparatively low Nixon profile during the 1970 college season probably can be attributed to the midyear elections. These had mixed results in the football community. Sam Huff was defeated in a Democratic congressional primary in West Virginia. Jay Wilkinson, former Duke All-American and son of Bud Wilkinson, the former Oklahoma coach who is the unofficial Secretary of Fun and Games for the President, was defeated as a Republican candidate for Congress in Oklahoma. Conservative Republican Jackie Kemp, who championed Nixon while quarterbacking the San Diego Chargers and Buffalo Bills, was elected to Congress from the 39th District of upstate New York. "There is a Republican President our surveys show is popular here," Kemp said before the campaign. "This is a Republican district, and I will not have to run against the incumbent. Machiavelli couldn't have come up with a better game plan." Although he had direct support from the White House, Kemp nearly blew it, which would have come as no surprise to his football critics. But with Bud Wilkinson in the White House and Byron (Whizzer) White on the Supreme Court, his election at last completed the checks-and-balances in government provided for in the Constitution.

Elsewhere, despite glowing allusions to Vince Lombardi in Italian neighborhoods, Republican candidates didn't have as much success as Nixon expected. The immutable laws of overexposure threw him for a loss when he tried to exploit his image as superfan. Humorist Art Buchwald explained how it happened in an interview with "Heinrich Applebaum, elite professor of political science at Moribund University."

The Republicans bought time on both NBC and CBS for a special political appeal by President Nixon to be aired between half times of all the pro football games in the country. It was a blunder of colossal proportions. . . . The silent majority is willing to listen to anything the President of the United States has to say six days a week. But Sunday they set aside to watch football. They don't want to hear about the Vietnam war, the economy, law and order, or violence in the streets. All they want to do is drink their cans of beer and watch two pro football teams kill each other. . . .

Up until half time the silent majority was willing to vote the straight Nixon-Agnew slate. But suddenly President Nixon appeared on millions of screens all over the country. The silent majority couldn't believe it. They were expecting to see a half-time show with a marching band and drum majorettes and baton twirlers and all the things that make pro football worth watching. . . . It takes a lot to get the silent majority angry. But this was too much. When you mess around with their football games on Sunday, you're hitting them where it hurts. . . .

Historians may conclude that that was a turning point, the beginning of the end of superfan as President, since he had already lost the loud minority. Political enemies, intellectuals and plain old sourpusses might have been willing to grin and bear his addiction to the games other people play—he being a ready-made excuse for their own addiction—but the country was traumatized by Vietnam and engaged in an orgy of agonized self-appraisal. In that context he came on like a coach who insists on running the same old play over and over no matter how often it fails.

In October 1969 about a quarter million citizens congregated on Nixon's doorstep in a Vietnam moratorium. He yawned that he had a football game to watch on television.

Six months later, in the wake of the invasion of Cambodia and the Kent State tragedy, a much larger congregation massed in Washington. At dawn Nixon walked among some of the students who had come hundreds and thousands of miles to bear witness, and he greeted them with small talk about football.

There was a flurry of activity in the nation's capital for weeks after that, indicating that government was listening. One theory had it that the President sensed the urgency of the young when he learned that many football players had joined campus protests. He might be a lot of things, but he didn't want to be the President who radicalized football players.

In another six months the abortive raid on a former prisoner compound in North Vietnam renewed domestic hostilities. A few days after the raid, at a Thanksgiving dinner in the White House, Nixon prophesied to a group of disabled veterans that we might even try another raid. "Sometimes you have to take them by surprise," he said. "It's like football. You run a play and it fails. Then you turn around and call the same play again because they aren't expecting it." Sure enough, there was another raid on another prisoner of war camp, by the South Vietnam Jayvees, and it failed too.

Wrote James Wechsler in the New York *Post:*

There are innumerable flaws in any game plan that equates Vietnam with a football field. For one thing, the other side has been playing this one for 25 years. . . . To believe that some remarkable new formation or some wily razzle-dazzle will suddenly destroy its will to resist is to succumb to delusion . . . One football phrase has grim relevance to the matter. In the waning moments of a bitterly deadlocked game a quarterback and his coach are frequently torn between the choice of settling for a draw or resorting to a desperate long pass (with the obvious attendant risks). In such interludes, reckless old grads will raise the cry: "Throw the bomb." One must hope that the fantasies in which Mr. Nixon pictures himself emerging as coach-of-the-year prudently exclude this final madness.

As odious as the Vietnam-football metaphor is, it is necessary to dwell on because the administration and the Pentagon unleashed a propaganda campaign applauding the success of the mission. Which was rather like applauding a well-designed, well-executed trap play that somehow didn't come off. The campaign resulted in the NFL going to the Pentagon Rent-a-Plane Agency, or vice versa, and getting free demonstrations similar to the one at the Super Bowl before several televised games. The operative word is televised.

At about this time, it should be noted, the American Broadcasting Company refused to allow the University of Buffalo band to put on a planned half-time show advocating the controversial notion of peace. It was, said ABC, too political. As for those planes, well, said NBC and CBS, it was non-political because everyone sympathized with the plight of the prisoners. Everyone did sympathize with the plight of the prisoners but, crucially, not everyone agreed how they should be freed; not a few thought that negotiations would accomplish what derring-do didn't. That, in 1970, was politics. So the pre-game glimpse of Jet fighters screaming overhead like winged horsemen of the apocalypse was as political as kissing babies and pressing flesh.

It isn't easy for fans who disagree with the policy of the President, or who resent the methods used to advance that policy, to find a positive side of his football show-biz promotion, but they could try this: the planes did fly low enough so we could clearly identify them as our own, and the pilot of the plane that peeled off, it has been learned, was Yossarian, out of Joseph Heller's *Catch-22*. It was Yossarian who discovered that the only way to get out of the Air Force was to be declared insane, but if you wanted to get out of the Air Force that proved your sanity. Glorifying a mission that failed was in the same great tradition.

(Showing his impartiality, Nixon plays political baseball too. He sent two pinch-hitters to the opening game of the 1971 season in Washington, Defense Secretary Melvin Laird and a Green Beret who had been a prisoner of war. Fans were reported to be restive during a speech by Laird. One dove dumped on him with a loud "Play ball!" The President could scarcely contain his joy when his son-in-law, David Eisenhower, got a summer job in the front office of the Senators. A Senator fan of long standing, Nixon decried their move to Texas after the 1971 season, and announced an instant switch in allegiance to the California Angels, near the Winter White House at San Clemente.)

Political football comes to us in all its plastic glory in pre-game and half-time rituals. The rituals usually are innocuous and godawful dull, and they are meant to be. For just as old-time basketball promoters closed the windows and raised the heat to sell beer, the game plan of football promoters is to drive us out to the hot-dog stands. The success of this ploy can be measured by the huge sales of bad overpriced hot dogs on cold rolls. Water commissioners also report that water levels dip noticeably at half time because bathrooms get such a heavy play from television fans.

With the Pentagon's Rent-a-Plane Agency at least temporarily sidelined after the prisoner-raid fiasco (its publicity campaign was grounded right after the Super Bowl), and its Rent-a-Band and Rent-a-Color-Guard agencies in a slump, the strong-side-left should be optimistic. But in politically charged times like these it still gets dyspepsia at the slightest hint of a martial air, wasting good dyspepsia. It even suspects it is being manipulated by military chauvinists when "The Star-Spangled Banner" is played. This is crazy. As crazy as the NFL, which, believe it or else, has a man in charge of The Star-Spangled Banner Formation.

Although the strong-side-left might be stirred or charmed by the British playing "God Save the Queen" at a spectacle or the theater, it assumes that our National Anthem is a reminder that Big Brother is watching this wholesome endeavor, whatever it is, with approval. Actually it's just a signal that the game is about to start, or, in case of riot, a means of restoring order. Look at it this way: they're playing our song.

In response though to strong-side-right complaints that athletes were disrespectful when they shifted nervously, or absentmindedly, or conspiratorially, during the Anthem, the NFL did appoint a Big Brother. A man at NFL headquarters was given the heavy responsibility of checking the official Star-Spangled Banner Formation—kickoff teams lined up on the 40-yard lines, at parade rest with helmets under arms, coaches and other players in the same stance on the sideline. Dave Meggyesy of the Cardinals was a conspicuous ideological shifter and one Sunday his coach, Charley Winner, stood next to him to find out if the complaints were true. But when the Anthem was played, Winner had to turn 180 degrees away from Meggyesy to face the flag. After Winner was fired that was cited secretly as an example of his inefficiency. And after the Cardinals were beaten by the Vikings once, a St. Louis sports columnist wrote that he could tell the Vikings would win because they showed greater discipline while the Anthem was played. (The Vikings weren't beaten again until the Chiefs stood ramrod tall for the Anthem just before the 1970 Super Bowl.)

Half-time shows seldom resemble Fourth of July celebrations any more but they have a long way to go before they resemble entertainment. Sparing all expense, the pros hire high school or college bands that toot and bong tired routines from 1950s musicals or variations on a theme of Stars and Midfield Stripes Forever, and every other weekend they bring us, direct from an automobile sponsor, a thrilling pass contest for nine-year olds. The Philadelphia Eagles and the Washington Redskins have marching bands of their own that play like the Redskins and Eagles play. The Eagles once entertained their fans by presenting the gala induction of thirty Marine recruits. There was no effort to give Dr. Spock equal time.

Owners welcome uninspiring and even depressing displays of patriotism at their games for various reasons. It's traditional. The acts are inexpensive. And it sells hot dogs.

It isn't bad politics either. Athletes have been idealized by the state as surrogate warriors since the Greek Gods thundered out of the heavens. Our way of doing it is by encouraging them to dodge the draft, through the National Guard and reserve commitments, so the game can go on. The owners, in return, can do no less than show their affection for such a bountiful system.

On occasion the political football takes a progressive bounce too. George Preston Marshall, who created the Redskins, was the last holdout against integration in the NFL. Not even the tide of enemy black players who integrated the Redskin end zone could sway him. But when informed that Congress would take a dim view of the lily-white Redskins playing in the stadium it was building in Washington, Marshall was struck by a vision of peace and racial harmony.

PRAISE THE LORD AND PASS THE FOOTBALL

Religion dovetails with political football when, in public ceremonies, it seeks to impose orthodoxy. Before a game, via a loudspeaker system, it simply imposes.

In some outdoor NFL temples fans get a sermon for the price of admission. On any given Sunday a crowd of sixty thousand is a powerful attraction for a messenger from above. In Miami the messengers, of all faiths, deliver embarrassingly long invocations. The players—some of whom may have been to church in the morning and in a team prayer five minutes before—begin to wonder if they missed their true calling. A few Baltimore Colts, their nerves on edge from all that pre-game psyching, accused their former coach, Don Shula, now with the Miami Dolphins, of trying to unstring them with a record-breaking invocation last season. Shula shrugged that he had nothing to do with it. Shortly thereafter the Dolphins designated, without luck, a man to keep invocations short. Sportswriters have a dollar pool going on their length. The champ is two minutes and four seconds, but, as we well know, records are made to be broken.

Joe Schmidt of the Lions, for one, objects to the exploitation of football players by the forces of righteousness. "Some people are trying to get ahead," he says, "by making the impression that we're a bunch of knights in shining armor."

The dressing-room prayer is another matter. Coaches sanction prayers for various reasons. It might not help, but how much can it hurt? The other coach does it and you can't let him get an edge. Maybe it will stimulate the selfless community spirit that drives men beyond themselves. Maybe a no-good scalawag will be reminded of his mother murmuring novenas and thus remember his plays better. And maybe the players will interpret the poetry of the Psalms as Mark Twain's "War Prayer" with its plea to "help us smite the foe, help us tear their soldiers to bloody shreds."

"All the guys kneeled down before the game to

say The Lord's Prayer," recalls Rick Sortun, formerly of the Cardinals, one of three pros who quit last year to pursue revolutionary goals. "When they were done everyone leaped up, put on their helmets and charged out of the locker room screaming, 'Let's kill the bastards.' "

Some teams even have their own chaplains. A priest in New Orleans goes to Saints' games with a large team emblem on his black jacket.

Jim Bouton, the baseball author, took note of the power of prayer in sports on his television show with this commentary:

In Nairobi, Kenya, one team spent $3000 on witch doctors last year. Sports leaders there have tried to discourage witchcraft as well as the practice of players painting their bodies with pig fat to ward off evil spirits.

Athletic teams in our country, of course, are much too sophisticated to travel with witch doctors and wear pig fat. Our teams travel with clergymen and wear medals.

In Africa when a team loses they get rid of the witch doctor. Over here when they lose, the clergyman stays and they get rid of the players. I like their way better.

Until World War I it was fundamentalist gospel that fun and games were the devil's doing. Playing hopscotch insured eternal damnation, playing football guaranteed the fire next time.

But as industrialization provided more leisure time, play was invested with the same virtues as work and sport gradually became a means to ever-lasting grace. Especially if you win. Vince Lombardi evoked God's word in one breath and in the next urged players to hate their opponents. George Allen of the Redskins is one of many coaches who have justified their excesses—when he was with the Rams, an assistant of his was discovered spying on an opponent's practice—with pious readings of God's will.

The Reverend Billy Graham has revealed exclusively that St. Paul was "an avid sports fan." A team of NFL archeologists can be expected to dig up this new version of the Ten Commandments at any time:

Thou shalt not covet thy opponent's playbook.

Thou shalt not pass deep into a zone defense.

Thou shalt not wear bell-bottom trousers.

Thou shalt not fidget while the National Anthem is played.

Thou shalt not stick to a game plan that doesn't work.

Thou shalt not negotiate through an agent.

Thou shalt not throw the football into the stands after scoring a touchdown.

Thou shalt not bear witness against thy teammate.

Thou shalt not rough the kicker or passer.

Thou shalt not use greenies.

The spectator sees a world gone soft and fat with affluence, populated by young men who wear their hair like girls and who scoff at athletes. The true football fan sees his heroes as respected, clean-living, fair-minded, team-spirited young men who typify the way they feel men should live and behave.

This compost of overthink and unthink comes to us from a think-tank called the Institute of Motivational Research. That spectators see a world gone soft and fat with affluence is unlikely, because they don't see themselves that way. To relate that and the youth rebellion of the mid-'60s to the popularity of pro football is as absurd on its face as some of the hair we see growing there. And the true football fan, who probably is raising a revolutionary under his own roof, sees athletes and their contemporary life styles moving closer to what he once considered revolutionary or immoral. But he doesn't give a damn as long as his team wins, and his attitudes may have changed anyway. As for clean-living and fair-minded ideals, such malevolent provocateurs as Johnny Sample and Ben Davidson have been adored in their home towns for what their fans view as zestful antics.

"There's a whole new generation coming in with new ideas and new dress," says Don McCafferty. "You've got to change with the times. Some of the guys have tried long hair and beards. I never made a point of it. I did emphasize that if they got cut on their chins our trainers are no professional barbers." The limitations of trainers, and the size of helmets, are eminently reasonable restraints on hair fashion or ideology. When Super Bowl hero Jim O'Brien was photographed playing tennis in shoulder length hair and a peace-symbol head band, McCafferty said he would take notice of it just as soon as it made his place-kicks veer off target. And the fans still love the Colts in Baltimore.

They didn't love Dave Meggyesy in St. Louis, but the Cardinals hadn't won anything lately. After doing the Funky Broadway to "The Star-Spangled Banner" and identifying himself as a radical and collecting an astounding thirty-seven signatures from his thirty-nine teammates on a peace petition, Meggyesy writes in his book *Out of Their League* that he was razzed by a) an apoplectic fan behind the Cardinal bench, and b) a banner in the stands that read "Big Red [Cardinals] Think Pink." If that was all the razzing he had to take, it was, relatively, a ringing endorsement for his politics. Mickey Mantle, the idol of America, used to get worse treatment from fans every day just for breathing.

Meggyesy and his teammate, Rick Sortun, and Chip Oliver of the Oakland Raiders announced their retirements early in 1970. While it was looked upon as a coincidental aberration by the NFL, it must have sent shock tremors into the heartland. Three rough, tough jocks who had passed the test of manhood on many a given Sunday, three young men who had played the game according to the rules and had been handsomely rewarded were walking out at the height of their careers to join the other America. They were rejecting fame and money, cherished values of the system. What are they smoking in the locker room these days? Are pep talks permissive too? Was it time to man the barricades?

Out of a thousand players in the NFL, all of whom at least brush-blocked their way through college, it figured that a few might join the exodus of cultural dropouts. To them that took character, pride, courage and high moral purpose. They were members of a generation challenging the country's values and priorities, members who through the naked competition of football had experienced the highs and lows of our system. Now they had decided that there had to be a better way and they wanted to find it or build it or pop it down their throats or something. Meggyesy gave up a salary of $35,000, Sortun $30,000, Oliver $25,000. That has to count for their sincerity. It certainly accounted for much of the shock and bewilderment in America.

For if they could abandon that stake in the dream, what about children with less to walk away from? Chuck Drulis, an assistant coach with the Cardinals, found out what. His son dropped out too after an injury ruined his shot at making the team as a rookie. When the Cardinals played in San Francisco later that season young Drulis, bearded, went to the team bus after the game. His father refused to acknowledge him.

Meggyesy, Sortun and Oliver had some things in common. They were lower-middle-class kids who grew up with strong bodies and modest athletic skills. They pushed themselves onward and upward by becoming what coaches call, with tears in their eyes, hitters. They played at big-time college football foundries. And they came to detest what Meggyesy branded the "dehumanizing" aspects of the game—the bed checks, the fear mongering, the view of opponents as hate objects to be destroyed, the discipline for discipline's sake that many coaches impose to assert authority and get respect they can't earn any other way. If "the spirit of the twentieth century is to convert man into a machine," as Norman Mailer claims, these nuts and bolts were reconverting. As it has for so many young people, the war triggered their rebellion. With the country in turmoil over Vietnam, they were deeply disturbed about being troops in what they consider a war game.

About "the war game." That ought to be buried quickly and mercifully, if not militarily. It is as much nonsense when used by the left as the right. Football is a game that has superficial resemblances to war in tactics and terminology. To that degree the metaphor can be humored. But when every off-tackle run is viewed as an imperialist thrust into Asia, when every kickoff is seen as a Marine landing in the Caribbean, it gets a bit paranoid. If they can play low-key football at Haverford, with the president of the college leading the cheers, and at Chicago U, with an old ice box crowned homecoming queen to symbolize all the frigid homecoming queens of the ages, it isn't the game that's the problem, it's the sanctimonious people who are exploiting it for personal, and not necessarily financial, gain.

The interchangeability of a handful of war and football terms—bomb, blitz, game plans, field general, etc.—indicts football about as much as the sexual-athlete jargon that also bothers Meggyesy—"opening holes" and "sticking it in there" —and let's not overlook the ever-popular deep penetration and that great new favorite, bump-and-run. Since Meggyesy is an advocate of so-called mind-expanding drugs, he might consider this from an interview with Timothy Leary, the guru of LSD, in the *Village Voice*.

> Hey, man, what position are you playing? I step back into the pocket, look downfield, and I see you in the clear. It's an easy touchdown, but instead of looking for the ball. . . . Sure I'm far out . . . all the way over to the sidelines on the left flank. I'll probably be cut down at the line, but meanwhile there's a hole a yard wide over left tackle. . . .

Abbie Hoffman, coach-quarterback of the Yippies, a member of the Chicago Seven, writes in *Revolution for the Hell of It:*

> What happened in Chicago can be viewed as a game. . . . One night I heard part of a live broadcast of a football game. "The guards smashed through the center, Taylor is now running around end, he's really flying —SMASH! They nailed him good. It's a fumble. . . ." I listened for about two minutes before I realized it wasn't the Battle of Michigan Avenue they were describing.

Yet Hoffman isn't uptight about football. He sees through the insanity of the strong-side-right and left in trying to capture or reject it. Of the lefts he says, "They're a bunch of peacenik creeps. Watching a football game on television, in color, is fantastic."

Is the violence of football a reflection of the violence in America and caused by America? It is, coos Meggyesy, "a reflection and reinforcement of the worst things in American culture." But there are countries as peaceful as Oz that have games as violent as football and countries with games no more violent than ping-pong that have periodic bloodbaths. (In Afghanistan they play a game on horseback that features such techniques as eye-gouging, groin-kneeing and slashing an opponent's face with a lead-loaded whip.) Oliver, like Meggyesy, says fans ought to be doing their own thing instead of watching other people play. No argument there, but many fans do both. And Germany, the most militaristic society of the last century, with no contact sport nearly as violent as football, is chock full of people who participate vigorously in their own sporting thing.

Meggyesy, Sortun and Oliver belong to separate strands of The Movement. Sortun is a socialist visionary. He informed Cardinal owner Stormy Bidwell of his retirement in a letter that started with a poem by Ho Chi Minh. He went on to say that Bidwell was his enemy and that he hoped they would be on the same side when the revolution comes and professional sports have been buried with the rest of capitalism. Jim Ringo, the all-pro center for the Packers for many years, once told Meggyesy that in football the Commies are on the other side of the line of scrimmage. Presumably Sortun, a guard, got his inspiration by lashing out at repressive capitalist pigs.

Oliver is into Charles Reich's Consciousness III with all ten toes and two pairs of jeans. He's a vegetarian and he lives in a commune and he runs a health-food shop near San Francisco. But he says, "I like the football part of it." There are contradictions in him that can be divined only by Al Davis, his former boss, who claims, "I hear there's dissension in the commune." Oliver has at once criticized the Raiders for drinking, eating meat and taking pep pills, because such devil's food makes it impossible for them, he says, to hit as hard as they can, and then he chomps on a hunk of banana bread and says, "The game perpetuates the illusion that we are not brothers. . . . What's the point of living if you are just trying to beat out the other guy? When I played football I was just turning people on to violence, competition and greed." Oliver was the likeliest of the dropouts to drop back in from the counter-culture, banana bread and all, and he tried to. He tried a comeback in 1971, as a safetyman (because he had lost so much weight), but he couldn't cut it.

Is competition bad? They agree that it can be overdone at the very least. Meggyesy devoted much of his book to detailing how athletes are corrupted by hypocrites in high school and college. Meggyesy, Sortun and Oliver are out to skewer the attitude expressed by George Allen that "The winner is the only individual who is truly alive" and "Life without victories is like being in prison." They would argue that that attitude itself is terminal and imprisoning.

Victories are essential to the professional, of course, but the attitude represented by Allen is a monstrous corruption of what games, competition, should mean on other levels. Competition can be fierce without being manic. It doesn't have to be "just trying to beat out the other guy" if it's done in the right spirit of fellowship. You can pick the other fellow off the ground or take him out for a drink after you've knocked his jock off. Or you can avoid becoming good at anything, which will help the morale of the other fellow while saving you time for more important things.

With the mirthless zeal of an apostate-convert, Meggyesy punctuates his odyssey from innocent to revolutionary with rhetoric like this: "When the revolution comes football will be obsolete," which is a safe prediction since there is no betting line on it, and this: "Nor is it an accident that the most repressive political regime in the history of this country is ruled by a football freak, Richard M. Nixon," which is bad history if nothing else. Yes, he thinks sports is the opiate of the masses. And he ends, after kenneling his dogma, by promising to join forces "with those individuals and groups trying to change this society."

George Sauer, star end for the New York Jets, son of a famous football player and coach, a $40,000-a-year man, took himself out of the game one year after the others. Like them, he objected to the military-school atmosphere and hate-thy-opponent mentality, although he admitted that the Jets were the best of all possible teams for him to be with because of the easy-going Weeb Ewbank. He was not into politics, but he had serious misgivings about the direction of the country and how football related to it. And he was a born free-thinker, having quit the Cub Scouts at eleven because "I didn't see any sense in getting gold stars for taking out the trash."

Sauer said, "Football's most obvious contradiction is its failure to teach character, self-discipline and responsibility, which it claims to do. There is little freedom. The system molds you into something easy to manipulate. It is a sad thing to see a forty-year-old man being checked into bed at night. It is personally embarrassing to realize you are a part of this. After years of acting and being treated like a seven-year-old, what else can you be but an adolescent?

"I like football. It is a framework around which you can see the dynamics of a player working together with other players, which can be a beautiful thing to watch. When people enjoy what they're doing it can be ecstatic. But the way it's structured, the intrinsic values of sport are choked off. It has been despiritualized, the profane applied to the sacred. Its inherent worth—doing it for itself, meeting challenges, the brotherhood on a team—is denied by treating the opponent as an enemy, not an antagonist. The game can touch you as a human being if you are permitted to touch others as human beings. But this is difficult when you have a Vince Lombardi type of coach hollering at you to hate the other guy, who's really just like you in a different colored uniform."

Sauer studied the origins of football for two years before reaching his decision to retire. He said, "The biggest clue I found is in football's history: why an elite segment of society (at Princeton, Rutgers, Harvard, Yale, et al) would invent and codify this game, which actually was more brutal then than it is now. Social Darwinism was being taught at the time—the survival of the fittest in society. The kids who played football were playing out the melodrama of the social theories of their parents. The political connotations today go back to those origins. Social Darwinism became American Darwinism, justifying anything we did [like Vietnam]."

Would it be cricket to point out that that same elite segment of society helped popularize baseball, playing club matches in white long pants before it spread to the masses? As Casey Stengel would say, you could look it up.

Meggyesy, Sortun, Oliver and Sauer, The NFL 4, are grappling with large issues, many of them beyond the scope of football. Prentice Gautt, a teammate of Meggyesy's and Sortun's, now an assistant coach at the University of Missouri, wrote a letter to C. C. Johnson Spink, editor and publisher of *The Sporting News,* suggesting how football must adapt to cope with some of the questions raised by the NFL 4. Said Gautt:

> . . . As the philosopher Bacon said, "He that will not apply new remedies must expect new evils." As coaches, we are seeing a different kind of athlete psychologically. No longer is he a glorified machine that can

separate himself from the rest of his problems. No longer can we expect the athlete to be docile and not ask questions. . . . It all revolves around how we (coaches) see people. Do we believe they are capable of self-direction, self-discipline and self-control or do we believe people are like children?

The easiest way to get forty human beings to march to the same drummer, most coaches insist, is to treat them like children. We can but wish The NFL 4 good luck and Godspeed in their earnest quest to change that and more, for as Vince Lombardi said on Honor America Day in 1970, less than two months before his death, "Patriotism is not something you wear on your lapel. It's not 'my country right or wrong.' I think you have to shout 'Hey country, let's turn around, let's do the right thing.' When I was young I fought for liberty and innovation. It's always been a function of the young to do that."

A moment of silence though for the terrible price The NFL 4 must pay. They will no longer be able to find sanctuary in dressing rooms during half time. They'll have to suffer through the tooting and bonging and flag waving with the rest of us.

If anything drives them back to the game, that will be it.

3. SNAKE OIL
AND PROFUNDITY

Albert Einstein revealed today, after years of secrecy, his formula for the forward pass. "E," he said, "equals MC²."

Einstein said the formula had come to him in his rookie year with the Oak Ridge Electrons.

"We were fooling around before practice one day," he said. "J. Robert Oppenheimer, the great end, Enrico Fermi, the center, and Bullets Teller, the halfback. I was kicking field goals. We kicked a lot of field goals in those days. Ran and kicked field goals, that's all we did. Well, I kicked one 40—45 yards and stubbed my educated toe. I sat down on the grass—we played on grass in those days— and took off my cleats and started to rub my toe, when it hit me."

"What hit you?"

"The ball—right on the head. Fermi centered it 15 yards over Teller's head and it hit me. I hobbled right over to the blackboard and wrote it down before I forgot it: E equals MC². E means end over end. I could kick a ball end over end 60—70 yards on kickoffs. C is the center. The center spirals the ball. But nobody ever put the two thoughts together before, that you could throw a ball 60—70 yards on a spiral. M was how you did it—with momentum, meaning you had to throw it like a baseball. Squared meant with twice as

much momentum as anyone thought of using before.

"Teller said I should call it The Bomb, but I think forward pass sounds nicer, don't you?"

THE NFL has a beautiful product. Running, throwing, jumping, catching, smiting, fighting. People can hardly get enough of it. Why then does the NFL have to oversell and hard-sell itself? Because the NFL has a problem, not unlike everyone else in football—what do you do the other six days of the week?

You keep yourself busy. Players consult with their mediums to determine if they will be emotionally up or down for the next game. Coaches construct elaborate game plans that they will abandon three minutes after the game starts if they have any sense. Television manufactures well-sponsored excuses to repeat action footage. Reporters report non-events. Tests all of character, courage, pride, high moral purpose and ingenuity.

The NFL's busy work is selling. No matter that it has become necessary to beat off the customers with forearm smashes and blind-side blocks. Selling is another name of the game. The NFL sells by pumping up its football with hot air. Ralph Nader should have them arrested.

The selling of the NFL-endorsed Ovaltine and NFL-endorsed chairs to watch NFL football is expected. The institution of a Hall of Fame to house the game's mythology—from Tom Matte's wristband to Sid Gillman's pipe to Jock Sutherland's jock—is expected. The mobilization of a TV cheerleader corps to enlighten the unwashed is expected. But the wholesale push to establish pro football as "A Game for Our Times," aided and abetted by intellectual jock sniffers who have discovered that the cosmos is shaped like a scrotum, is going too far. It is a pile of parvenu. It is a crock of self-importance.

Pro football has become a very big thing in the last fifteen years, and there is no abiding mystery about that. The pro football boom parallels booms in urbanization, affluence, communications, leisure time and education—and other sports. More people in more cities with more money and more time. More communication through television and more identification with the sweet Saturdays of youth through the more common experience of high school and college.

The pro football phenomenon might be worthy of cosmic deep-think if it was an isolated phenomenon. It isn't. It is, simply because it is so well suited to television, in the forefront of a long noisy parade.

College football, despite competition from the pros that has buried it in most urban centers, continues to thrive and grow.

Baseball, so often dismissed as a rural-age anachronism, is alive and well. Attendance is at record levels, television revenue exceeds football's. The day-to-day caring and hysteria in Boston, Chicago, New York, Detroit, Cincinnati, St. Louis and elsewhere in recent summers is still unmatched in the NFL anywhere this side of the village of Green Bay.

Pro basketball and ice hockey are enjoying booms much like football's. Basketball, because it is an ideal game for TV with its controlled energy and tight area of play, is making the biggest advances today.

Automobile racing has had the most spectacular rise in attendance of all sports over the last two decades.

Golf and tennis, indoor track and outdoor trotters, none of them the subject of dazzling think-tank studies, have gone boom, boom, boom as spectator attractions.

Etcetera, etcetera, etcetera.

But the NFL, with six days of every week to contemplate its navel and its commercial possibilities, has its own exotic theories to explain its wonderful self. Take a swig of your NFL-endorsed Ovaltine, sit down in your NFL-endorsed television chair, and brace yourself. Some exotica from *The First Fifty Years,* a $14.95 chronicle produced by the "Creative Staff of National Football League Properties, Inc.," with comments:

> Other societies have had their symbolic wars. The gladiator in the arena, the knight at the joust, provided entertainment while performing the skills of battle. In her turn, America has created her own vicarious warfare, nurtured by the technology that is this land's hallmark and tuned to the needs of this people's spirit.

The war metaphor is the most common and most glib of the attempts at dissecting the anatomy of football's body and soul. It received intellectual support from William Phillips, a literary critic, who expanded on the theme in *Commentary* magazine:

> Football is not only the most popular sport, it is the most intellectual one. It is in fact the intellectuals' secret vice. Not politics, not sex, not pornography, but football, and not college football, but the real thing. Pro ball is the opium of the intellectuals. . . . Much of its popularity is due to the fact that it makes respectable the most primitive feelings about violence, patriotism, manhood. The similar-

ity to war is unmistakable: each game is a battle with its own game-plan, each season a campaign, the whole thing a series of wars. Football strategy is like military strategy. The different positions, each with its own function but coordinated with the rest of the team, are like the various branches of the armed services. There is even a general draft. And one is loyal to one's country—according to geography and the accident of birth . . . pro football legitimizes untamed feelings . . .

Nobody wants to deny an intellectual his amusement in these tortured times, but this tidy toy-soldier vision can be kicked end over end over end. For football, from a fan's view, is among the least intelligible and therefore intellectual games in man's sweaty arsenal. (Baseball, for example, is much the deeper intellectual board game for fans, because its tempo and geometry enable strategy, happenings and personalities to be defined so vividly.) And in truth football fans have become largely callous to the violence, in some measure because they have been distracted by so much mystical snake oilmanship.

At the end of the 1971 season the NFL commissioned a broad survey by the Louis Harris polling organization that refuted the NFL's own pretensions on violence. The responses to a variety of questions—"In your daily life, what does watching pro football do for you?" and "What do you like best about pro football?", etc.—indicated very clearly that the overwhelming majority of fans related primarily to such non-violent goodies as "entertainment, enjoyment, relaxation, recreation, fast-moving play, spectacular play execution, favorite players, uncertainty of outcome and good passers." Less than 10 percent of the fans identified hitting as the name of the game. This isn't to say that the other 90 percent or more are flower children who would find the game as entertaining and enjoyable and relaxing if there were no hitting at all—if it was touch football—but it must mean something.

What is amusing about the war metaphor is that it used to be applied to baseball of all things, a game that football fanatics consider as warlike as a picnic in the park. A philosopher named Morris Cohen once wrote: "I am ready to urge the claims of international baseball as capable of rousing far more national religious fervor than the more monotonous game of armaments and war." He suggested that Prussian generals would make love not war if they had baseball teams to root for.

In 1924 George Bernard Shaw covered an exhibition between the Chicago White Sox and New York Giants in London for a newspaper. Anticipating anthropologists and psychologists who would make much ado about games, Shaw pecked out this mocking lead:

It is a noteworthy fact that kicking and beating have played so considerable a part in the habits which necessity has imposed on mankind in past ages that the only way of preventing civilized men from kicking and beating their wives is to organize games in which they can kick and beat balls.

Hence cricket and football in England and baseball in America. Women beat their husbands and children for want of an energetic alternative.

Musical nations like the Irish resort to instruments of percussion to satisfy the irresistible impulse to hit something. The Ulster drum has saved many a Catholic from a broken head.

Behaviorists Robert Ardrey (*The Territorial Imperative*), Desmond Morris (*The Naked Ape*) and Konrad Lorenz (*On Aggression*) and all-around genius Marshall McLuhan have made us curiouser and curiouser—and skepticaler and skepticaler—about the role of sports in society. They have underlined its primitive origins and motives and, like psychologists and sociologists have done since we came down from trees, its individual and group therapeutic values (which are now being challenged by psychologists and psychiatrists). But none of them have singled out football as the one compelling sports outlet (except as a television vehicle, by McLuhan). That is, their generalizations, co-opted so neatly by the NFL, are as apt for other games. The NFL, by appropriating lines such as Lorenz's "Sports contains aggressive motivations and its main function today lies in the cathartic discharge of aggressiveness," is determined to puff itself up with profundity, as players puff up their chests with anabolic steroids.

What the NFL seems to suggest is that going to football games neutralizes the aggressions of fans, aggressions that would otherwise break out in olive-pelting skirmishes at cocktail parties, or in more Vietnams. This is not only counting but psychoanalyzing the angels on the heads of pins.

Most of us will continue going to and playing games because they're fun, because they are good theater and because they are what Satchel Paige would call social rambles. But we are comforted to know that in our small way we have helped civilization survive, such as it has, by expending our aggressive energy sixteen to twenty any given Sundays a year. It is amazing that we muddled through until, say, 1965, before we realized that we had better get season tickets and color television sets lest we commence to bite our neighbors' necks on the way home from church. As for the other thirty to thirty-five weekends of the year, and all those Tuesdays and Thursdays when we feel like smashing our bosses, make the martinis dry or the marijuana groovy.

Football as a reflection of the big business-team play ethic has been explored too. In an article in *The New York Review of Books,* Murray Kempton quoted from a study by The Harvard Program on Technology on the professional athlete as a model of performance in industrial managers:

> At the risk of some exaggeration, football can be considered as a paradigm and symbolic expression of the organizational character in action. . . . (The football player's) syndrome of traits—which can be called the game character—is of inestimable value for building both winning teams and organizations that can maximize a certain type of innovation and material production. The game character thus appears to be an essential resource for an industrial society.

Fair enough. The drudgery of the assembly line, glamorized, is the drudgery of the football line. But Kempton notes that "The game character does not seem easily transferable. When professional athletes turn to management, they are anything but innovative. . . . The value of the football player's syndrome of traits to building a winning team in management is indicated by the recollection of one of [Joe] Namath's partners in enterprise: 'The board meetings were a joke; we had one in his apartment while he was taking a shower and he'd just holler "yeah" from the bathroom while there was a vote.' "

Pro football, it seems worth remembering here, did not make it big until it became a wide-open spectacular that depends on one-man brilliance and a two-man connection as well as eleven-man teamwork. The teamwork is implicit, but on every team there are exceptional players and success usually comes in direct proportion to their numbers and positions, and their ability to break creatively from the assembly line.

Returning to the NFL's creative division, we next find this:

Pro football rose to dominance in the 1960s, at a time when the United States experienced a social-political crisis unparalleled in its history. Crowded into increasingly unmanageable cities, governed by a seemingly unreachable bureaucracy, given an unwanted war in Asia and the upheavals of racial and educational factions at home, distraught by continuing violence and tragedy, the nation fell into a bluesy period of introspection its leaders could not assuage. In such a mood the nation turned gratefully to a sport whose driving excitement not only filled certain needs more felt than acknowledged, but did so in patterns well suited to this complex, scientific society. . . . Many sports attempted to expand, but they found that a discriminating public rejected losing teams created from expansion drafts. Only one sport, professional football, grew continuously and soundly . . .

Barely concealed in this pretense at social significance are two historical inaccuracies. 1) Pro football's rise preceded the national malaise described here, which began with the assassination of President Kennedy in November 1963. (For which, incidentally, the NFL was the only public spectacle that went on with its schedule, reasoning with increasing fervor over the years that it was necessary to right the ship of state and all its distraught passengers.) 2) And by that time the American Football League was closing out its fourth season in a comically bitter fight for survival with the NFL. Two and a half years later the leagues merged, adding ten teams to the NFL. Expansion in pro football has been as much of a haphazard hassle as it has been in baseball and basketball, some franchises making it quickly, others surviving only because television was underwriting the show. Major league hockey has had the only sound, planned expansion policy, creating a parallel division of new teams that wasn't consistently overmatched.

The best football teams are the closest teams. . . . Any good game, and the pros rarely play poor ones. . . . On live television, football players act out the crucial moments in their lives. . . . Money cannot buy his devotion to the game; there are easier ways to make a living. . . . It is very hard for a man to play unless he has been brought up in it, as he has in his language.

These fragments are lifted from *The First Fifty Years* because they are typical of the abstractions and hyperbole that pro football deals in, partially because the nature of the game is such that more often than not the only thing you can be sure of after a game is the score.

The best football teams are the teams with the best talent and the best coaching, and when you have both you win and when you win there is closeness among the players. Closeness is a result more than a cause. . . .

There are poorly played games all the time and the fans are beginning to recognize them because they have been so glutted with games. Their enthusiasm is regenerated by a rooting interest and by gambling. . . .

Fans seldom relate to "the crucial moments in their lives" because individual achievements often are as obscure as the individual players hidden under all that padding. . . .

Their devotion to football is not necessarily greater and may not be as great as the devotion of a mechanic to automobiles. They stay in the game because they can't do anything else as well, or that is as exhilarating, or as rewarding. They hang on for as long as they can, and then many of them coach. Linemen, the steam shovels of football, probably could be bought off faster than any professional athlete for a decent white-collar job. Some have retired prematurely, more would if they could make it financially in the real world. Four players in their prime have retired in the last two years. No other sport can make that statement. Is it possible that football is a game out of step with the times? . . .

Cornell Green made it with the Cowboys after not competing in football for four years in college. Soccer-style place kickers are recruited from Tasmania. No other sport is populated by so many disconnected athletes.

The NFL also promotes its pretensions in the programs it sells in stadiums throughout the league. You are as likely to find a quote from Friedrich Nietzsche as Ray Nitschke in them. Even Ralph Waldo Emerson and e.e. cummings have marched to the NFL's drumming. Dig this: "The cover photograph of the Cleveland Browns resembles nothing so much as the prehistoric monoliths of Stonehenge. . . ." And this: "The data here is graphic imagery. The image, like the language, is esoteric and only just short of abstract . . . an essence has emerged as a distortion of active forces. The game, mobile and plastic, has thus been stretched through the eye of the computer."

Where have you gone, Bulldog Turner?

Football, says the NFL, in case we haven't

noticed, is an art form. Are the Houston Oilers and the Atlanta Falcons going to play an exhibition in the Louvre next season? No. But Leroy Neiman, the former artist-in-residence for the Jets, has played out his option. And Ernie Barnes, who sees the game in his oils as a grotesque battleground, is high on the draft list of the Cowboys.

Love's Labor

Perhaps there is a place for art in pro football. And for music and literature. Mike Reid, a defensive tackle for the Cincinnati Bengals, has given piano recitals with symphony orchestras. Bernie Casey, as an end with the Rams and 49ers, was a professional artist and published poet. To soothe his savage breast, Dick Butkus, the fearsome linebacker of the Chicago Bears, was going to try Shakespeare.

Linebackers, particularly middle linebackers, because they are in on so much of the action, get reputations as uncouth, unruly citizens. In defense of the breed, Mike Curtis of the Colts once said, "I'm an animal on the field and a gentleman off the field." And Ray Nitschke of the Packers has done television commercials for a hand lotion. Still the notion persists that they are legal muggers. Butkus, perturbed because people seem surprised that he speaks the mother tongue, once planned to do a recitation of Shakespeare on a record. It didn't come off. This, forsooth, is to take a bard's-eye view of him in action.

Smashing through a cordon of blockers: "Doomsday is near; die all, die merrily."

Roman Gabriel preparing for the Butkus blitz: "I have not slept one wink."

Butkus eying a double-team block: "Here come a pair of very strange beasts, which in all vogues are called fools."

A rookie end after running into Butkus over the middle: "This learning. What a thing it is."

Burying a runner: "Down, down to hell; and say I sent thee thither."

Third down and three yards to go, Butkus crouches warily, looking for a tip-off on whether it will be a run or pass: "I do perceive here a divided duty."

Butkus ponders his game plan: "Flout 'em and scout 'em, scout 'em and flout 'em. I do begin to have bloody thoughts."

He intercepts a pass: "Flat burglary as ever committed."

It's an end run, he gives chase: "Sweep on, you fat and greasy citizens."

Leroy Kelly after Butkus flattens him: "I do desire that we be better strangers."

Butkus: "Oh! It is excellent to have a giant's strength."

Kelly: "But it is tyrannous to use it like a giant."

After Kelly tries again, Butkus rises from under a pileup: "Lord, what fools these mortals be."

Kelly: "The beast with many heads butts me away."

The coach speaks of his star: "A very gentle beast, and of good conscience."

The opposing coach: "Who can control his fate?"

Butkus explains his philosophy: "I must be cruel, only to be kind."

Fran Tarkenton scrambles, Butkus growls: "Play out the play."

Tarkenton flees to the sideline: "He is an enemy to mankind."

Butkus belts him anyway: "A hit, a very palpable hit."

Tarkenton beseeches an official: "To be or not to be?"

Butkus is grief-stricken: "I have lived such dishonor that the gods detest my baseness."

Tarkenton: "The play's the thing."

Butkus: "I am alone the villain of the earth."

Tarkenton: "Truly, I would the gods had made thee poetical."

Butkus, menacingly: "The better part of valor is discretion."

Tarkenton: "And when he falls he falls like Lucifer."

Butkus offers to shake hands and forget the incident: "All's well that ends well."

Tarkenton agrees: "I will praise any man that will praise me."

After the game Butkus submits to interviews.

"Great game, Dick."

"Greatness knows itself."

"Why do you play this base game anyway?"

"The purpose of playing . . . was and is to hold the mirror to nature."

"Is that why you're laughing?"

"They laugh that win."

"But you didn't win."

"Praising what is lost makes remembrances dear."

"But you didn't lose either. It was a tie."

"Sweet is the kiss of a sister."

4. MEN ATTEND, WOMEN COMPREHEND

"I don't know what happened," Napoleon Bonaparte *said through clenched teeth. "We met our Waterloo but I'll have to check the films to find out why."*

The legendary field general and his French Eleven fell before an all-star team of British, Germans and other Europeans. Observers agreed that a failure of nerve, when he refused to stick to the ground and started to throw recklessly, cost Napoleon dearly. "We thought we could hurt them with bombs," he said.

Another theory had it that Napoleon's gallant team was exhausted after last week's game with Russia in a blizzard. Napoleon admitted there might be something to that.

"It's hard to play at an emotional peak week after week," he said. *"I'm not taking anything away from Wellington's club. They're a good club, soundly coached. But we were down. We didn't play our game."*

Wellington felt that Napoleon's comeback had been doomed from the start. "He was great in his day," he said, *"but Napoleon is too short to stand in the pocket today."*

PHILADELPHIA. Franklin Field. Eagles vs. Steelers. Sun-dappled day in September. Field plush-green. Yard-stripes and sidelines chalked yellow.

She: They look like dandelions.

He: No, love, the Eagles and Steelers.

She: Dandelions. Look.

He: The dandelions, love, play in Detroit.

She: I mean they *look* like dandelions: running around, blowing in the wind, the colors.

The Eagles wear green uniforms with green helmets. The Steelers wear yellow with yellow helmets. On that green-and-yellow field ...

He (to himself): Good grief, I'm looking for trap plays and zone defenses and she sees more of what this is all about than I do.

And that is petrified truth. Women generally do see more than men at football games. Which is why it is imperative for men to take their wives, girls, mistresses, mothers or daughters to games. Men's heads are cluttered with so much nonsense that they frequently miss the best part of the show. They need womenfolk as guides and interpreters.

On a day when the home team is losing on merit or when the weather is bad, for instance, the men dismiss the quarterback as a spastic and question the ancestry of the coach. The women look around for amusement, and find it. The players—boys rolling in the mud—huddle on the sidelines in parkas that women may see as the height of masculine chic. Perhaps an emotional lineman stands uncovered shaking a fist at the fates, his hair sensationally unkempt: God, she says, or thinks, the size of the neck on him, and the bulge in those calves. Sex can be the name of the game too. The scoreboard, blinking its magical mystery code, may be too mysterious for her to decipher, but she knows the half is coming to a close because the band stirs and then groups behind the end zone. Unconsciously she has hooked into a quarterback's wavelength: "I aim for the tuba," says Don Horn of the Denver Broncos, explaining how he throws the ball out of bounds when his receivers are covered.

If the lady is Elinor Kaine, the lady sportswriter, or one of her readers, he or she may latch on to some fascinating trivia. Like that fellow with the towel sticking out of the back of his pants for his teammates to try to dry their hands on. "The team maid," Elinor calls him. If he's the center she might regale you with a rundown of NFL centers you won't get in the scouting reports—their love lives, hangups, feuds, etc. Then a recitation of this Ogden Nash ditty:

> The life of an offensive center
> Is one that few could wish to enter.
> You'll note that that of Dick Syzmanski
> Is not all roses and romanski.
> He centers the ball, he hears a roar—
> Is it a fumble, or a score?
> What's happening he can only wonder,
> He accomplishes amazing feats,
> And what gets photographed? His cleats.

The grimmer nonsense of the pro football mystique narrows men's field of vision to the line of scrimmage. It ranges from the pretense of being able to foresee or understand strategy that is often obscure to the players themselves, to the illusion that being able to spout jargon and spot the difference between an X and an O in a meaningless play diagram qualifies you as an expert. This is like being distracted from a psychedelic light show by examining a fuse box. The male of the species is cursed by a compulsion to know how things work and when it's overdone, as it is in football, it undermines the primary sensual pleasure of watching the game.

There are three basics to football: the spectacle, the violence, the forward pass. Men see about three-quarters of one of them, on a good day. Women, their antennae more receptive and their field of vision as wide as the stadium, see a lot more.

College football games are our most colorful sports spectacles because students can be hip, zany and creative in their enthusiasm. Crowds at pro games tend to be humorless and when the home team hasn't been winning enough lately, which usually is the case, they can get sullen and mutinous, as a coach once said. Still, pro football can give us a spectrum of fine madness, from insane traffic jams to the sound and fury and the fustian and wham and back to the traffic jams. As for the half-time shows, they're likely to be two-touchdown underdogs to a chorus of Jew's harps.

To men that is something to be endured, to be suffered for art's sake. To women it is the string of pearls on the basic black dress.

Women see and sense the violence of football for what it is too, and, bless their sweet hearts, they may even like it. Men have become largely callous to the violence, which is the core of the game, because their heads are into the mystique of strategy and jargon and deep-think, and the imperative of victory. (The three plays called by superfan Nixon last season were a screen pass, an end-around, and a forward pass, not exactly your basic knock-the-hell-out-of-them Green Bay sweep.) "The love of violence, the dedication to violence," says Gary Pettigrew of the Eagles, "is what this game is about." Yet the bulk of the fans, the men, seldom connect to the violence directly.

Their connection is indirect: the comment that this team has a good front four, that that linebacker is tough, that the blocking is lousy. Have you ever heard a fan discuss the intensity of the violence in football? It isn't likely. A woman's eyes follow a groggy lineman off the field for a second or two longer than a man's. She winces when a runner is stopped for no gain or a quarterback is nailed; he second-guesses the call. About the only time they are on the same frequency is when a pass spirals toward a moving target of fingertips. The pass, with its potential for instant rapture or despair, is a sight dug so viscerally and freely that not even strategic pretense can interfere with it. But when the receiver is throttled, she shudders; he checks the first-down chain.

Except for those rare body-hurtling collisions in an open field, the hitting blends into the grass. From a distance the players resemble so many toy boxers in a penny arcade. Most fans are too far away or too involved with the flow of the game to see, hear, smell or feel the hitting for what it really is. It is as abstract as the pain in a newspaper photo. They are looking at the romantic hurly-burly of actors on a screen.

Paul Brown has said, "I've known women who thought football was worthless and brutal. They just don't understand the sport and don't understand the nature of the male. Most of the big collisions don't hurt. The players are young and strong. Anyway the fact is that young men enjoy it."

Young men do enjoy knocking each other around—before football it was the custom at many colleges for entire classes to test their manhood on each other in freestyle scrums—but while it's true that individual collisions don't always jar them, sometimes it's because they're numbed out of their skulls. The cumulative impact is shattering. Not even television, with its repertoire of closeup lenses, picks up the vibrations of the field shaking under the thundering herd, of muscles trembling and smacking. The instruments needed to record them are a seismograph and an oscillograph. "If a man doesn't get hurt," says Larry Wilson of the Cardinals, "he hasn't been playing hard enough." By the fourth quarter linemen are playing on instinct revived between shifts by smelling salts. Leroy Neiman, the artist who has been sketching prize fights for twenty-five years, said after his first season of football, "They're asked to give too much." Put a woman on the sidelines and she might faint or run away screaming. From ground level those uniforms getting up a fraction slower than usual, those helmets tilting back between plays, they are people swallowing hard through the hurt, girding for one more charge. A man's entire perspective would be shaken from the sideline, as though he had been pushed into the bull ring. It isn't just a ballet or a game of chess from there.

The violence escalates to the megaton level on kickoffs, when twenty-two bodies try to knock off twenty-two heads. The incidence of injury on kickoffs is roughly eight times what it is on scrimmage plays. Stan Isaacs, sports columnist for *Newsday* on Long Island, New York, would make kickoffs a game alone:

> For those who think pro football is the greatest of spectacular sports I'd like to call attention to a game I call "Annihilation." It's not for sissies. Annihilation is like football, but without the dull parts. It's a game of kickoffs. Each team takes turns at kicking off and receiving—and may the better team survive.

For variety there could be a one-on-one head-to-head collision between, say, Calvin Hill of the Cowboys and Mike Battle of the Jets, called "Self-destruction." Hill and Battle are football's foremost leaping maniacs. When there is no place to turn, or run and hide, they leap into people. They could start on the goal lines and meet at the 50. They wouldn't even need a football.

Actually the general spectator insensitivity to the violence of football is best dramatized on kickoffs. Despite their glamour, their potential for a thrill, the expectations they raise, very little happens on the average kickoff in terms of yardage gained. There are nine or ten kickoffs per game, of which six or seven are returned, one or two beyond the 25-yard line. In a good year 1 out of 300 returns results in a touchdown, in a bad year 1 out of 500. But everyone follows the beautiful end-over-end flight of the ball on kickoffs, followed by a quick scamper to the 23—while a human demolition derby is taking place upfield. Demolition is the name of that game.

Each of us brings our own sensibility and neuroses to the stadium, enabling us to find whatever we want there, from fun and games to hero and scapegoat and even to catharsis and the fount of essential, infinite wisdom. Norman Mailer has found the relationship between the quarterback and the center, well, absorbing. Henry Kissinger, assistant coach and grand defense strategist in the White House, is said to be an all-pro grandstand quarterback. Good luck to both of them. The thing we have to remember is that none of us knows what's really going on out there, and that knowing is unimportant. Seeing and feeling are important.

Because, for the fan, if not for the coach, pro football is by yards and yards the least intellectual game there is.

A hockey crowd is a football crowd without the pretense. Strategy, shmategy. The game is a blaze of color: swift, violent, explosive. Which is more than enough to involve you.

A basketball crowd in a basketball city, pressing around the court, is aware of the game's schoolyard subtleties and stratagems to a sophisticated degree impossible in football.

And a baseball crowd is geological ages ahead of a football crowd, because baseball is easier to follow and anticipate, and because the statistical records and daily exposure define athletes as athletes and personalities.

The problem in football is trying to assign individual responsibility, trying to sort out what happened from that clamor of bodies. The problem is compounded by the fact that even should you be able to determine precisely what happened, chances are that some of it was set into motion and commotion off the field.

Doug Atkins, the mountainous defensive end, once hinted at this when he said after a game in which he was conspicuously unspectacular, "They tell me to go left, I go left. They tell me to go right, I go right. I just go wherever they tell me."

Atkins may have been saying any one of six things. He may have been saying that the coaches had him so confused that he didn't know what was going on, that their game plan read like the stage directions for *No, No Nanette*. He may have been saying that the offensive tackle opposite him wiped him out, or that he was double-teamed because the tackle next to him couldn't penetrate across the line of scrimmage if they were playing the Daughters of the American Revolution. He may have been saying that his team's offense was so terrible it never gave the defense a chance to rest or a lead to work with. He may have been saying that he had to play it safe because the linebacker behind him was a disciple of non-violence. He may have been saying that he had a hangover. Who knows? Not even Doug Atkins perhaps.

Try to analyze a simple incomplete pass. Was it incomplete because the quarterback panicked in the face of a rush? Or because he didn't get enough time? Or because he was following orders from the bench? Or because the receiver didn't go where he was supposed to go? Or because the quarterback didn't know where the receiver was supposed to go? Or because the defense anticipated his target and the quarterback didn't see another open man? Or because a speck of dust got in someone's eye or a gust of wind came along? Or did the quarterback throw away the ball deliberately because of any or all of these reasons? There are five or ten passes thrown away in every game, but only when the ball is thrown into the fifteenth row of the bleachers, or into a tuba in the band, can fans be reasonably sure that that is what's happening. And who knows, maybe the quarterback has a thing for the tuba player.

Fran Tarkenton, who has a low rate of interceptions, threw two of them in one game against Dallas last season. It developed that one pass play had been called by an assistant coach but ambushed by a linebacker who knocked down a back who was supposed to go out and occupy a safety-man who made the interception. The second one was caused by a receiver who zigged when he was supposed to zag. Meanwhile Tarkenton had been hissed at, threatened and otherwise abused by nine million people who saw the game on television.

The successful running play has its own set of rational possibilities. Did the line open a hole a pregnant sow could have waddled through? Was it guaranteed to work because one coach out-smarted the other coach, or himself? Did a line-man pull when he should have plowed ahead, only to pull a key defensive man out of the path of the ballcarrier? Did a linebacker react too slowly or a cornerback not at all? Was the defense over-shifted to protect against another runner, or the pass? Or did the runner make everyone from the coach to the blockers to the quarterback look good by his individual ability? All of this reason-able speculation explains why play diagrams might as well be maps leading to Captain Kidd's hidden treasure for all the enlightenment they provide.

As the preacher said, many attend, few compre-hend. But innocence is its own reward and a state to be devoutly wished for in the football degener-ate. Since the dark abyss of the line of scrimmage, like the football mind, is impenetrable anyway, the way to enjoy this brawling game and dazzling spectacle is simply to look at it simply.

There is some hope that a process of unlearning is taking place. That the fan, bombarded with so much unintelligible nonsense by the NFL through the media, especially television, is rebelling, tuning out. Gradually it may be sinking in that nobody knows exactly what's going on out there. When players talk about pride, character, emotion and momentum all the time it begins to dawn on us that perhaps we are dealing with athletes who are as confused as we are. This realization may induce a state of melancholia among many men, but think of the dividends in expanded consciousness.

The first casualty may be the game plan. A game plan is a guide to attacking and defending against your opponent, based on relative strengths, weaknesses and tendencies. Coaches and, in some places, computers digest scouting reports and excrete personality profiles on the opposition: what they like to do in every imaginable situation, what game plan changes *they* make from week to week, what the philosophy and quirks of the coach are, etc. Insofar as this procedure keeps the coaching staffs occupied, alert and off the streets at night, and insofar as it convinces the players that their coaches are working hard and therefore contributes to their own peace of mind and concentration, it is harmless and occasionally beneficial. The problem is that it contains the seeds of its own destruction.

Having invested so much time, money, energy and faith in the game plan, which is the climax of the whole scouting-film-computer cycle that starts with the player draft, coaches sometimes cling too long to it. "Giving up the game plan" may seem like a sign of weakness to a coach, of losing control, of defeat, a reflection on his genius. So, perversely, many a game plan has resulted in a defeat because the coach refused to believe the evidence of his eye: that the damn thing wasn't working, possibly because the other coach didn't do what he anticipated, possibly because the crazy players and the funny ball wouldn't pay attention to him. In the 1971 Super Bowl the Cowboys ran to their left on first down six times and made over two yards once; Tom Landry explained that they kept at it, moth- and flamelike, because it should have worked, meaning it was in the game plan. Any fan could have told him there's a death wish in there someplace.

Conversely, the game plan being a reflection of what his team does best, some coaches may not cling to it long enough. But more often it becomes a kind of Linus security blanket, and veteran quarterbacks are forced to jerk it away, leaving the coaches naked and frazzled. Sonny Jurgensen and Fran Tarkenton are two of them. "You can take all your sophisticated game plans and forget them," says Tarkenton. "I don't have my game plan until I go on the field and see what the other side is doing. This mystique about game plans is bull."

If game plans aren't sacred anymore, can a return to the age of innocent enjoyment be far behind?

THE PRO FOOTBALL MISSTIQUE

Not every woman in America stood up and cheered when pro football became an indoor sport on Mondays, too, last season. Tuesdays, Wednesdays and always might be next if the television ratings hold up. Perhaps that's what provoked this letter to and response from advice-to-the-lovelorn columnist Abigail Van Buren:

Dear Abby: My husband is a good man. He supports us, he loves us and he's true blue. But I have a gigantic problem. I am so jealous of football I could scream. I have heard and read all kinds of consoling pearls of wisdom, such as, "Just be glad he's home to watch those games," or, "Don't fight him, join him." But weekend after weekend he sits with his eyeballs glued to the television set, with a portable radio beside him listening to another game. All he ever says to me while the games are on is, "How about something to eat?" I really wish I could stir up an interest in a bunch of men falling on top of a ball just so I could share it with him, but I am sorry to say, it doesn't move me. This might sound humorous, but it's really a last desperate plea for some kind of fresh advice on how to change things. I've had it.

—Mary

Dear Mary: If you can't find something to do while your man is enjoying his favorite sport, you need more help than I can give you in a letter. Bake a cake, clean closets . . . What needs changing at your house is not your hubby's hobby, it's your attitude.

Let's hear it for Abby. If Germaine Greer starts advising the lovelorn she could spread havoc for football. But let's hear it for Mary too, because the suffering of millions of Marys yielded an Elinor Kaine as surely as the suffering of millions of women yielded a Susan B. Anthony. Elinor Kaine was inevitable. She was inevitable because if pro football invades every third living room in the country, pretty soon an Elinor Kaine is bound to drift out of the kitchen, curious about the noise. Then, upon hearing all that exotic jargon about zig-outs and odd-man defenses, and scanning the much less complicated action on the screen for a couple of minutes, she is going to decide she knows more about it than some of those fool announcers. That's Elinor Kaine.

Somebody would have had to invent her if she hadn't materialized out of a New York living room eight years ago. Pro football was already taking on the trappings of a pseudo-religion, fully understood only by the Dalai Lama and the big-mouth in the lumber jacket who sat in front of you. Elinor undertook the mission to deflate the game's mystique. She began to send a weekly news-letter to her many friends, called *Line Back,* which achieved a national circulation in the thousands before she retired it last season.

Elinor went after the flatulence of the NFL with a sweet vengeance. She disguised her gibes at pretentious fans with advice to the ladies. "Jump up after every running play and say, 'Did you see that pulling guard?' It doesn't matter if you saw him or not. There's always a pulling guard. When there's a punt always say, 'What a punt.' It works if it's a good punt or a bad punt."

Using a vast underground network of inform-ers—bartenders in key pubs, assistant coaches, coaches' wives, trainers, her father, sportswriters, club secretaries, bookies, a rabbi in San Francisco—Elinor collected gossip and notes that brought to life some of the bloodless personalities in the game. Example: "Wally Hilgenberg of the Vikings still lives in Detroit in the off-season and rents his house to Roger Shoals of the Lions. On Saturday before their game last week Wally called up Roger and said he wanted to come over, no doubt to make an inspection for neatness. But

Roger was so tight that he didn't want to talk to Wally at all (it wasn't the fact that Mrs. Shoals hadn't vacuumed in months and the house was a mess). In the game Hilgenberg ran out of bounds near the Lion bench and Mike Lucci, who is one of Wally's best friends, punched him in the mouth."

Reading Elinor you would have learned that Ken Gray of the Cardinals once brought a rattlesnake into the dressing room to stir things up, that Gale Sayers doesn't dance a step on the dance floor, that Al Davis refused to pay for the rented television set of a hospitalized Oakland Raider, that Cleveland owner Art Modell turned the lights on at Municipal Stadium one night to have a place-kicking duel with actor Walter Matthau. Also that Bubba Smith sends all his paychecks to his mother, and puts his size 14½ cleats on first and then pulls his pants over them. And that Ron McDole of the Redskins, formerly with the Buffalo Bills, didn't allow motorcycle racing through his haunted house at the Bills' annual Halloween party.

At a game Elinor is a multi-media experience. She is equipped with a radio to listen to a second game, a portable television face up at her feet in a shopping bag to watch a third game, and binoculars to spy on anyone worth spying on in the ball park. The scoreboard adds an extra dimension. And the thermos of martinis she shares with friends and neighbors doesn't hurt either. She carries on a running, giggling commentary as developments on the field, on the radio, on the television and on the scoreboard unfold. The Packers are behind? She knows about some wild parties they had in Green Bay last week. The Bills are ahead? She muses that owner Ralph Wilson sure needs the bread to pay his alimony. Down on the field the Jets score again on the Patriots, reminding her that the Patriots use Esteé Lauder's Aramis cologne in their dressing room, and they're sure going to need it today.

None of this is cosmic, but that's the idea. Neither is football. "I enjoy reading *Line Back*," said artist Leroy Neiman, "because it's non-functional."

If millions of Marys yielded an Elinor Kaine, it doesn't necessarily follow that Pat Palinkas has arrived on the scene because of a million Elinors. They are one of a kind. Pat showed up with pads in 1970—football pads.

A schoolteacher in Tampa, Florida, Pat Palinkas was one of those dedicated wives who held the football for a husband who wanted to be a professional place kicker. When he went for a tryout with the Orlando Panthers of the Atlantic Coast League, she went with him. They were hired on the spot.

Shortly thereafter, in an exhibition game, Pat Palinkas knelt on one knee waiting for the snap from center. But she dropped the ball and the meanies on the other team dropped on her. "I'm out here trying to make a living," said the 235-pound linebacker who got to her first, "and she is making a folly of a man's game." In that moment of truth she had. Unshaken, she got up as though she had been doing calisthenics on her bedroom rug and tiptoed off the field, grinning sheepishly. So much for 235-pound linebackers.

The Pálinkases came through on their next try and later Pat was encouraged by her mother. "Don't worry," she said. "Football is just like housework. You get used to it."

The female perspective had its finest hour or hours, at one Super Bowl, when a reporter didn't get to the game because he had been waylaid the night before.

"Gee," he said, sitting up in bed, his 50-yard-line television seat, "I never knew that watching the Super Bowl could be so much fun."

"Honey," his ladyfriend replied, "you're in the Super Bowl."

5. N. TANGIBLES
AND
MO MENTUM

The Sioux took no prisoners in the Little Big Horn Bowl yesterday. Playing for steady field position, punting on third down, they led the U. S. Cavalry into the biggest trap play ever.

"We had the horses," said co-captain Crazy Horse.

"We had the bulls too," said co-captain Sitting Bull.

Custer, the bold Cavalry quarterback, was not available for comment. "He lost his head," mourned General Terry, the coach.

According to Terry, the game plan was to play conservatively until the Cavalry could mass for its off-tackle offense. Instead, Custer tried a naked reverse and the Sioux were waiting for him.

"We win because we have character," said Crazy Horse.

"We win because we have pride," said Sitting Bull.

"We have confidence in ourselves," said Crazy Horse.

"We can go all the way," said Sitting Bull.

Terry was disappointed but not discouraged. He said the Cavalry had the nucleus of a good team. "And don't forget," he said. "We'll have the top draft choices."

Scouts, coaches, general managers and psychologists are trying to find out what's inside football players' heads. Wish them luck. They need it.

Mayo Smith, baseball manager, once said, "Open up a ballplayer's head and you know what you'd find? A lot of little broads and a jazz band."

That's baseball. Football is more complicated. There are intangibles in there too. The N. Tangibles are the troublemakers.

Consider this random sampling of pro football's N. Tangibles game:

1. The Rams and the Giants played their last regularly scheduled game of 1970 in New York. The Rams would have to win and the 49ers would have to lose to the Raiders, hours later in San Francisco, for the Rams to make the playoffs. The Giants needed a victory to assure themselves of a playoff berth. Big game.

The Rams were slight favorites although sign readers east of the Mississippi read the signs so favorably for the Giants that you would have thought Mayor John Lindsay wrote them. The Rams had lost the previous Monday night to the Lions, and we all knew how difficult it was for a team to get itself together for a game six days later instead of seven. On top of that the Rams would lose an extra day of practice or sleep or both traveling. On top of that George Allen was coaching what was believed, correctly, to be his last game with the Rams. That was a certain sign of something, if we only knew what; it didn't sound good for the Rams. On top of all that, the Rams did not have full control of their destiny while the Giants, aiming for their first shot at post-season money and glory in seven years, and playing in front of the home folks, could win it for themselves. The Giants would be higher emotionally if not wider physically than the Rams.

But the Rams won 31-3 and the game wasn't as close as the score indicated.

And then the metaphysical void.

Some Giants advanced the Theory of Up and Down to explain the shellacking. The Rams were Up, the Giants were, by definition, Down. This is one of football's most popular and trickiest theories. (A euphemism for Down is flat, as in Joe Schmidt's classic post-game urinalysis, "We were flat as a plate of piss.")

A team that is Up is a team that theoretically plays as well as it can. A team that is Down plays at less than its best. Thus everything that happens on the field can be explained, or rationalized, abstractly. When a player says, "They were Up," he is saying in effect that his team's poor play was dictated by uncontrollable fates, not by the superiority of the other team. The tricky part is that only losers advance the theory. When they win it isn't because they were Up and the other guys were Down, because that would be saying in effect that they weren't masters of their own fate. When they win they are just naturally better.

The Rams thought they were better, of course, but they had an equally fascinating theory to expound: that it's not what you do as much as what you say that makes the difference. The Giants, according to this theory, had said too much before the game. Allen, who in his book *Inside Football* advised coaches to "Never use the news media as a propaganda or psychological tool," had contrived a campaign to boil the competitive juices of his players with newspaper clippings. One showed a group of Giants laughing. As any head coach could plainly see, they were laughing at his team. In a second clipping Fran Tarkenton was quoted as saying that it was fine with him if the Giants had to play the Rams in the big one. As any head coach could plainly see, he was mocking his team. Did the Rams buy this high school ploy? Sure they did.

This raises some interesting questions, starting with: could the Rams read? And: what if the losing coach used clippings too? (The Giants' dressing room was festooned in bed sheets with signs urging every manjack to die for dear old team, each player signing it in blood or the equivalent in ink. This proved that bed sheets weren't as stimulating as newssheets and indicated repressed guilt feelings for bed-wetting.) And: why did the Rams or the Giants need more incentive than a chance to make the playoffs? And: is this another example of coaches playing with themselves?

Deacon Jones was one of several Rams to vouch for the clippings. The Rams wanted to go out there and show the Giants they couldn't put them down like that, he said. It was unprofessional to cast aspersions on a pro's pride. And more like that.

Then someone asked Deacon Jones what the score would have been without the clippings.

He grinned and said, "Thirty-one to three."

Nearby there was another X-ray vignette of homo sap jock's head. The Raiders had taken an early lead over the 49ers and one Ram said, turning away from a television set, "Al Davis [the head Raider] wants to kick their ass."

Twenty minutes later the 49ers were leading 28—7. "That sonofabitch Davis," said the same Ram. "He's dumping."

That's one.

2. The Dallas Cowboys won their division title that season by winning their last five games in a row. Here are the reasons they gave for their resurgence:

Ralph Neely, tackle: "We grew up." John Niland, guard: "We found something we didn't have—character." Rayfield Wright, tackle: "The guys have a feeling for each other." Leroy Jordan, linebacker: "We had to turn to each other for friendship." Chuck Howley, linebacker: "We just kind of went out there and played football."

As far as it can be ascertained, no player attributed the team's comeback to any of the following:

The Cowboys, who had lost all of their games to teams with winning records, did not play a single winning team in those last five games.

Duane Thomas, brilliant rookie runner, gave the Cowboys a ball-control offense after replacing the injured Calvin Hill.

Tom Landry began to send in the plays for Craig Morton.

Landry, whose sophisticated theories of offense and defense have been criticized by players as confusingly complex, simplified both his offense and defense.

That's two.

3. Strange things happen at the end of the season when some players on also-ran teams are just trying to get out in one piece. The also-ran Bears beat the also-ran Packers in their last game. A few Bears credited the victory to a seventy-minute pep talk given to them early in the week by a successful businessman named W. Clement Stone, who spoke to them about Positive Mental Atti-

tude. "I wish he could have spoken to us before the season started," said quarterback Jack Concannon. Little did he realize that the Packers had enlisted J. Paul Getty and the Aga Khan in their losing cause.

That's three.

4. Jim Marshall and Paul Dickson of the Vikings went on a snowmobile expedition in Montana after the season. They got lost during a blizzard and nearly froze to death before they were rescued. One elderly man in the party died. A fifteen-year-old lived through it and was told by Dickson that he had shown character that would stand him in good stead in the future. Marshall said he owed his own survival to "the lessons of determination and competition one learns in football."

A few days before this incident, three scrawny college students—members of the math team at best—were found alive and well in the snows of Vermont after getting lost for several days in a storm. They allowed that they had been inexperienced in such travails but they had huddled together and survived. If they thought it made them better human beings, or if they thought that the thousands of hours they had spent practicing quantum physics had enabled them to come through, they neglected to say so.

That's four.

So what is there about football that turns grown men into babbling idiots? What is this character they are always patting themselves on the back about? And courage and momentum and pride? Is there a magic elixir that separates the winners from the losers? Can you buy it in the drugstore? Do you pour it on Wheaties?

Vince Lombardi said, "This is a game for madmen" and Muhammad Ali said, "There sure is a lot of crazy people in this world" and maybe that's all you need to know. But this would be an awfully short chapter to leave it at that.

One thing we have to remember is that football players get hit on the head a lot. So much that some of them claim that in the course of a career they lose an inch or two in height, the cartilage between their vertebrae getting battered down. Scout's honor.

Second, most players are so occupied by their small piece of the action and so preoccupied with themselves and their fears that they really have no conception of the big picture of the team or the game. "They're probably the most misinformed bunch in pro football," said Mike Holovak, former coach of the Boston Patriots.

Third, they lean to the abstract, as George Orwell said of politicians, in "defense of the indefensible." If you've been hit on the head, and you don't know what happened, and you don't want to reveal anything of substance because it might indict yourself or a teammate, you two-four-six-eight obfuscate.

Fourth, it is the game. Alex Karras reminds us

that unlike baseball football doesn't require many split-second skills of timing. A football player, he says, needs size and attitude primarily, speed in some positions. In football the idea is to hit people rather than balls, and some people hit back.

That is why coaches try every device imaginable, and some unimaginable, to stoke hotter and hotter fires in their players. Football is such a beastly game, they believe, that the only way to get professionals to practice and play at a proper level of intensity is to bang a drum loudly and constantly. But where is the pride in an athlete who needs that sort of stimulation? And the character? The only sure way to get an athlete to perform at or near his peak is to surround him with good athletes and a good coach and a good organization that will pay him for his trouble. The ability and the attitude are there, formed, for the coach to know what to do with, not to inhibit. Vince Lombardi did the job with Paul Hornung the day he moved him from quarterback to halfback in a system that utilized his talent. George Allen, who is very big on N. Tangibles, once said of a rookie, "He almost regurgitated at half time, and it took Gatorade and smelling salts to revive him. He showed me he's got character." Incredibly the kid didn't make the team.

Last, the football player mouths these abstractions because high school and college coaches like

Allen have fed them to him like a circus animal trainer slipping biscuits to dancing bears. Run four hundred laps. Good boy. Here's a character biscuit. If we win the game you get a courage and a pride biscuit. And if we go undefeated we bite from the biggest biscuit of them all, the team-desire biscuit. In this way players are trained to play hard and viciously, which is what the game is about, and also made to feel that that makes them better citizens, which it doesn't. They are not mutually exclusive, but the notion that football-type character equals citizen-type character is Orwellian.

Character, courage and similar goodies are shorthand for relentless aggressiveness, for being a tough competitor. Nobody has bestowed character awards on Joe Namath, yet he plays on two badly damaged legs and he gets off the ground to challenge the defense again and again and he is a winner. Nobody bestowed character awards on Johnny Sample, but he was an outstanding player on three championship teams. Coaches would eagerly recruit and sing the praises of King Kong if he could count to five. To illustrate what some football players are made of, Warren Johnson, professor of health education at the University of Maryland, told the following story in *Psychology Today:*

> . . . Athletes draw the line between accept-
> able and unacceptable aggression at differ-

ent points; . . . I interviewed eight men, all of whom wanted to be more aggressive in their games. To find out just how much they wished to be, I put each into a deep hypnotic state and asked him whether he would like to receive suggestions that would make for the most aggressive possible behavior short of poor sportsmanship. All eight said they would. I asked each how he would react to suggestions that would make him totally aggressive, to the point of not caring if he hurt other players or broke the rules of the game. Two athletes were so alarmed at this that they immediately began to emerge from their "trances." Four others stated emphatically that they did not want such suggestions and would not follow them. But the last two, a champion swimmer and a professional football player, said that any increase in aggressiveness would be welcome, the more savage the better. This, they assured me, was the nature of the competition. Not too surprisingly, both men were hot-tempered and prone to get into fights of the barroom-brawl type, and they had more severe aggression/guilt problems than the other six. They were also far more successful than the others as competitive athletes.

Which suggests, accurately, that many pros would sell their souls to the devil for a lick of his

fire. Else why would they—on top of the character, courage, pep talks and newspaper clippings —need amphetamines, those much-popped evil greenies, to play the game? (One star halfback, given a suppository by a trainer, swallowed it. Force of habit. They'll try anything.) If you didn't know better you would think these brutes have to be pushed onto the field.

Courage too, like character, is a widely abused word. In the verbal overkill of this sporting life it may apply to anyone from a batter who stands close to the plate to a golfer who goes for the flag to a lady who wears gold pants at Wimbledon. In football, players who have a "reckless disregard for their safety" are called courageous. That takes in everyone but the place kickers, although under Hemingway's definition—"grace under pressure" (what we call poise)—maybe they qualify best. But all these seem like narrow applications of so noble an attribute. Dave Meggyesy, Rick Sortun, Chip Oliver and George Sauer, The NFL 4, who proved their physical courage many times, showed a courage much rarer when they gave up football for their ideas.

The last of the red-hot N. Tangibles is Mo Mentum. The cliché mongers on television have transformed Mo into a Holy Mo, a supernatural energy force who helps winners win again and again and again—until they lose. Teams that win are said to have Mo in their lineup, meaning things are going well. "We've got momentum" is one of the staples of the NFL. Invariably players heading for a playoff invoke Mo's name to explain why they expect to keep winning. It seems a pity to have to remind them that the other team has Mo too.

Once the game is under way, Mo goes sixty minutes, for both sides. He is neither loyal nor disloyal. He is merely a positive who can't stand the negative. He plays sixty minutes and he changes sides, it is said, with every whim of fortune, like a true front-runner. If the Steelers recover a fumble—zap, Mo becomes a Steeler. If the Oilers intercept a pass—zap, Mo is an Oiler. That's what they tell us.

That's not what Virgil Carter, quarterback for the Cincinnati Bengals, tells us, however. Carter got a master's degree at Northwestern University where he co-authored a paper, "Operations Research on Football," that may make Mo as obsolete as the drop kick. With the aid of his wife, who coded and computerized twenty thousand plays from the first half of the 1969 season, Carter examined the importance of field position in football. He reached two conclusions.

Carter found that players are not motivated or emotionalized by Mo when they recover a fumble or make an interception. Whatever they feel, whatever tingle of anticipation lights up their toes, the significance of a turnover is that it gives the ball to one team close to the other team's goal line. And the closer it is the better chance it has to score.

Why didn't anyone else think of that? Because it's too simple.

Carter also found—quite the opposite of conventional wisdom—that a team that scores a touchdown does not have Mo, or either of his cousins, on his side. "One of the highest motivating forces to rally a team," he says, "is to have the opponent score." The probable reason: it becomes urgent to retaliate. A team that has been nursing a lead or playing conservatively in a tight game is more likely to open up its offense after it is scored on. Like Willie Pep, who would be content to jab his way to an easy decision until the other guy got fresh and hit him, whereupon Pep would clobber him.

Now that's pretty serious stuff. If Mo is a myth as a supernatural force—and the fact that, generally, a team can turn itself on by opening up its offense indicates that it is—where does that leave eMotion? It is there of course. But where? How is it measured? Most often by the final score. Like the coin of the realm, a very rare phenomenon has been devalued by inflation—an inflation of language. The rare phenomenon of adrenalin's becoming the name of the game, of some magic spark igniting people to extraordinary feats, has been devalued by a din of supernatural gibberish.

Ballplayers and coaches themselves are starting to line up with Carter to expose occultists.

Johnny Unitas: "The best way to play this game is calm and collected. As far as I'm concerned it's a thinking man's game, not an emotional game."

Tommy Prothro, replying to a reporter who asked him if a touchdown the Rams scored gave them an emotional lift: "I guess it did. It also gave us seven points."

Larry Csonka, explaining why he got a team ball after a Miami victory (supposedly an emotional thrill second only to being presented with a first child) : "Breaking my nose was the key. You sacrifice a pint of blood and you get the team ball."

It would seem that professionals, who by definition are supposed to perform at a high standard, who have jobs at stake and families to support and egos to bulwark and teammates to join in common cause, have enough natural stimulation without the artificial jive of coaches and trainers. Perhaps that's why people are looking into their heads.

THE X-RAYS SHOWED NOTHING

Timothy Leary, when he was a clinical psychologist at Harvard, used to tell his colleagues that they would be wise to get rid of their white mice, to chuck their mazes into the Charles River, and continue their research at Fenway Park in Boston. Ballplayers, he reasoned, were playing in the controlled environment of a game, under all sorts of human conditions—the pressure of coming through at critical times, fighting slumps and minor ailments and bad weather, etc.—and their performances could be calibrated. What better way to find out what's going on in homo sap's head, and get an afternoon in the sun while you were at it?

That fanciful vision has grown, Topsy-like, into a movement to plumb the depths of the football psyche. Professional teams employ psychologists to supplement the physical side of scouting reports and find shortcuts to player motivation. Psychologists in turn are using football to try to fathom the mysteries of aggression. It's a marriage made in Dr. Frankenstein's laboratory. In the fantasies of coaches it can't be long before football players are running around with wires sticking out their skulls, coaches manipulating them from master panels.

The plunge into the murky psychological pool follows the leap into ice-cold computerized scouting, swimming in the abstract after diving into the concrete. A look at current scouting procedures first.

The Dallas Cowboys are the acknowledged champs of the computer circuits, spending $200,000 a year pumping information into brain machines at Stanford University. That is in addition to the estimated $250,000 the Cowboys and other teams invest in talent recruiting. The Cowboys have consistently innovated in this area and, having won five division titles and two league championships and one Super Bowl in their twelve years in the NFL, they have been widely copied. If a team won with a warthog at center, twenty-five other teams would send out expeditions to Africa the next day.

The Cowboys were the first and remain the only team to successfully draft basketball and track stars who hadn't played football much or at all since high school. The object: speed. Cornell

Green, a basketball player in college, became an all-pro cornerback. Bob Hayes, the Olympic Gold Medalist, did play football in his senior year in college, but the Cowboys drafted him as a "future" pick (a draft category no longer in use) when he was a junior, and he became an all-pro end.

When the trend toward foreign soccer-style place kickers was in full flower, the Cowboys sent out what they called a Kicking Karavan. They scavenged the countryside looking for Walter Mitty kickers in tryouts. They found two who eventually played elsewhere in the NFL. They had to trade for one of their own.

The emphasis on intelligence in players was one of Paul Brown's many bright ideas. But Brown uses simple who-is-buried-in-Grant's Tomb?-type tests to weed out only hopeless mental defectives, believing as behaviorist Robert Ardrey does, that: "Without in many cases the benefit of a registerable I.Q., whether the athlete has the mental capacity to rattle about in the interior of a thimble or to strain the capacities of a ten-gallon hat, he will with equal facility learn complexities of plays, subtleties of movement, intricacies of rules and regulations to baffle an Einstein." The Cowboys don't limit themselves to Rhodes Scholars, any more than they pay much attention to their so-called character ratings—they drafted Duane Thomas No. 1 despite N. Tangible reports that scared off other teams, and they hang on to him despite his neurotic behavior—but they insist on higher minimum intelligence standards than the opposition. And they will keep on doing so until some magnificent hunk of tackle with a head as empty as the Cotton Bowl in June is available.

The intelligence thing and the computers got notoriety when Calvin Hill had an outstanding rookie season in 1969. The Cowboys had drafted him first out of Yale, which might have been Mrs. Ames' Finishing School as far as most scouts were concerned. "The big computer could handle anybody," said an assistant coach, Jim Garrett, now with the Giants, "and they were putting in information on his height, weight and speed. It was going along nicely—click, click, click—when they put in his I.Q. Poof. It blew up the computer."

Garrett says there are many NFL greats who couldn't play for the Cowboys because of Landry's intricate system. This may explain why he had to simplify it to get to the Super Bowl. The Jets and the Chiefs, who started in the same year as the Cowboys, 1960, and the Vikings, who started a year later, got to the Super Bowl before they did. The trouble with systems, like game plans, is that teams get locked into them and don't know how to get out.

The Cowboys, for example, say they don't draft for positions, rather they draft the best athletes as rated by the computers, regardless of positions.

Stay-moist power

We'll be right back after this word from Rapid Shave . . . .

Marion Motley—former Cleveland Browns' great (he's the one on the left)— and his team, the Daredevils. It had to come to this.

Equal rights for women has become a major political
concern of the pros. Joe Namath heads the movement
in the NFL.

Nobody gets closer to news sources than football writer Elinor Kaine.

Women have a different perspective on pro football.

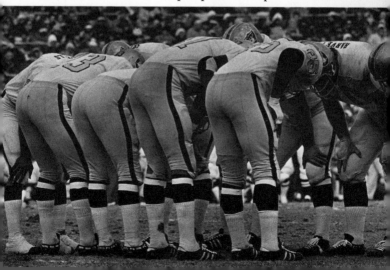

Now a message from Gillette from Len Dawson and Joe Kapp....

Thank you, John Brodie, and now back to the game....

So in a three-year period from 1968-70 they drafted four ends in the first two rounds, and none of them has made it. They may very well get locked into the I.Q. Box too. Gil Brandt, personnel director of the Cowboys, says their quarterback must have a 120 I.Q. or higher. Aside from the quarterback problems the Cowboys already have, that means they could use Charley Johnson and Frank Ryan, who have doctorate degrees, but they'd have to pass up Johnny Unitas and Joe Namath, who win championships. True, a computer once beat a famous scientist at chess, but the computer didn't get hit on the head for fifty-eight minutes and then have to make a decision or a throw that would decide the game.

Ultimately the machine is at the mercy of the scouts, who feed it information, and the organization, which sets its priorities. The Cowboys think an outside linebacker should have a 4.9-second speed in the 40-yard dash, the Jets think 5.1 will do if the player analyzes plays quickly. But scouts have problems measuring standing people much less moving ones. The Eagles drafted Richard Harris, a tackle from Grambling, on the first round last year. Their records indicated he was 6-5. After they made the choice a scout told them he was 6-3. A week later they pinned him down at 6-4. Three years ago Bob Stein, a linebacker at the University of Minnesota, was clocked in 4.9 seconds by one group of scouts, who listed him as "quick and agile," 5.1 seconds by a second group, which listed him as "stiff with no agility," and 5.0 by the Kansas City Chiefs, who drafted him on the fifth round. Thus are empires built.

The dilemma that short-circuits scouts, organizations and machines is the great athlete who is unstable. Even the machines love them. Who could not love the aptly named Joe Don Looney? The Giants drafted Looney first out of the University of Oklahoma in 1964, although he had been kicked off the team in mid-season. Looney was a large muscular swift halfback; in short, the type of athlete who brings out the psychiatrist in every coach. Looney stayed with the Giants for one hectic month. He is remembered for going left when told to go right, for having furious battles with mechanical dummies that kept knocking him on his brains, and for his cunning arguments. He was fined for missing bedcheck, and he argued that he had gone to bed early the night before so the Giants owed him time. They assigned elder statesman Y. A. Tittle to explain the facts of pro football life to him, and Looney convinced Tittle that bedchecks were ridiculous. That was the first hint that he might be smarter than anyone knew. The second was when he said, "I never met a man I didn't like, except Will Rogers." He spent parts of the next few seasons with the Colts, Lions, and Redskins, usually wearing a coach's patience thin just when he was about to get a chance to play. In Washington he did play some, and it turned out that that was all he could play, some. Maybe he knew it all along.

Joe Don Looney might get the highest marks for aggression, which brings us in full stride back to the new psychological probings into football and scouting. It can begin with the Cowboys reporting that the average I.Q. of top NFL cornerbacks is 95 (undoubtedly excluding three Jet cornerbacks, one with a degree in entomology, a second who writes poetry, a third the only Harvard man in the pros). But two psychologists reported in *Sports Illustrated* that "emotional stability and mental toughness" are the necessary attributes of a cornerback. What a team does is look for the best cornerback it can find and draft him. If he falls into any or all of these niches, fine. If he doesn't, they'll create a new niche for him.

Paul Brown's innovation in psychological testing is being carried to an extreme too. Many teams today are using testing services that provide psychological profiles of their players, purpose being to check them out for quirks that may help a coach in handling certain players. In most cases where the coach learns something he learns that he ought to be more patient. That suggests the coach should be taking the tests.

The St. Louis Cardinals did give tests to candidates for their coaching vacancy in 1970. One candidate, Jerry Burns, an assistant with the Vikings, refused to take it. "I would be for the test if it would help defenders get to the passer," he said.

Charley Winner, the former head coach, said that the Cardinals gave tests to their players with disastrous results. Winner told Dave Brady of the Washington *Post:*

> We wanted to try to evaluate the unknown. We had the veterans tested first because we wanted to see if the results of the test would match what we already knew about the players. They did not. The tests showed that some of our best athletes should not be playing football, yet some had made all-pro. The tests indicated that some of our players were not aggressive who were. One was Chuck Walker. I knew he was over-aggressive. . . . The tests could not determine which players would work hard, or what was inside them.

The problem is that there isn't necessarily a direct correlation between psychological aggression and physical aggression. Some of the least hostile sweethearts on the planet are prizefighters. Some of the most hostile louts are dress designers. Psychologists and psychiatrists are coming around to the thinking that the drive to physical activity doesn't have to be an outlet for deep-seated aggressions, a commonly held belief. There are an increasing number of football players, evidently, who can play well and feel a sense of accomplishment at throwing a vicious block, without experiencing emotional jollies. It is done, says Warren Johnson, "in the manner of an expert dancer or gymnast—or soldier or hired assassin."

Alan Stone, a psychiatrist who played football at Harvard, divides players into three categories in an article in "Motivations in Play, Games and Sports":

1) The player who dominates his opponent by skill or force without any "specific devices toward hurting the opponent." This player's aggression is "instrumental rather than destructive," to achieve a goal. "As such it seems to represent one example of a useful process of integrating aggression in an acceptable personal and social manner. Such players are often respected by teammates and show outstanding qualities in other areas as well."

2) The player who uses destructive techniques to dominate his opponent. He is a good player although he probably has a little less skill than the top players. "The superego may develop a layer in which primitive acts of aggression are condoned."

3) The player who "functions out of viciousness for its own sake" because, though big and strong he is basically incompetent. "The group code justifies this to the individual despite the fact that on occasion it may be highly nonfunctional for the team."

Experiments being conducted may yet illuminate the amazing three pounds of brain that helmets, with mixed success, try to protect. Scientists at the University of California have been able to tell in advance whether a wired-up chimpanzee is going to make the right move in a game of ticktacktoe. How long will coaches be able to resist the temptation to wire their quarterbacks? A scientist at the State University of Stony Brook (New York) is doing research on brain waves that may provide clues on how to psych oneself up to maximum efficiency. A psychology professor at the University of Massachusetts is trying to relate experiments that show that people increase speed as they near a goal to the claim of Robert Ardrey that defense stiffens as offense threatens its territory and goal.

Maybe they all should study Casey Stengel. "I used to play football without a helmet," he says, "and that's how I got this way."

6. ST. VINCE

Charles Darwin, head scout for the Beagles, who have had the rookie of the year in the NFL for six straight years, says their success proves his theory of natural selection.

"We have graduated from scouting by computer and stopwatch," Darwin says. "We have discovered over the years some universal truths about football players that we employ in what we call natural selection. We look for natural athletes, that is, athletes who are naturals for the various positions.

"For example, in offensive guards we look for players who are too small for tackle, too slow for fullback, too meek for defense. When you find a player like that you can be certain he's a natural guard.

"Safety man is another interesting species. A safety man is too slow to be a cornerback, too small to be a linebacker, can't catch the ball well enough to be an end. There is only one position for such a player: safety.

"The easiest position to fill by natural selection is quarterback. In a quarterback we look for a player who can't run, block, catch or tackle. If he can't do these things, we feel we can teach him how to throw. And if he can't throw, he can kick or even hold for the kicker.

"There is, we have found, a natural position for everyone in professional football."

A teammate of Vince Lombardi's at Fordham once said, "Vince didn't like the courses in religion we took, so he created his own religion." Paul Hornung told the story of Mrs. Lombardi complaining one night, "God, your feet are cold," Lombardi replying, "You may call me Vincent, dear." Norm Van Brocklin called him St. Vince.

The coach as deity is an ancient and trusted metaphor, mocking in tone, guaranteed to get a cackling response at awards dinners. The trouble was, people didn't cackle at Vince Lombardi. They thought he was peeled off a fourteenth-century fresco or discovered in a basket in the bulrushes of the Nile.

Vince Lombardi didn't invent a new religion but he did improve on an old one. It is called Winning.

Winning is what Vince Lombardi was all about and in the context of the professional football boom and the climate of the times it made him a great man in America. The Packers won five championships in ten years under Lombardi, more than just succeeding the Browns of the '50s and the Bears of the '40s as the ruling dynasty. In the '60s there was television, and more television, and that made a difference. Because when things started to come apart at the center of the society, America drew up mythical teams. Joe Namath represented the Nihilists and Vince Lombardi represented the Moralists. Lombardi did not reject the role.

Vince Lombardi was a hard man coaching a hard game with a hard code, and he coated it in moral rectitude, in terms of God, family and team, duty, responsibility and discipline, and respect for authority. Not a bad list but all too often used by coaches as more of those animal biscuits to get athletes to sit up on their hind legs and follow by blind unreasoning obedience. Still, it was music to the ears of those who were deaf to the wails of their children. There were a lot of people who thought Vince Lombardi was a monastery in Green Bay, Wisconsin, where they could send their long-haired sons to get them straightened out. Somebody should have told them what Bobby Dodd, the marvelous former coach at Georgia Tech, once said to a parent who turned over her son to him with the hope that the boy would, as they say, learn some discipline. "You give me a good boy," Bobby Dodd said, "and I'll give you a good boy back."

On his deathbed in August 1970, Lombardi

was reported to have hallucinated, "Namath—football is bigger than you are." Which, if apocryphal, seems dramatically correct. Lombardi had once said that Americans emphasized "genius above discipline, which is never going to work." But when it came to his own geniuses, like Paul Hornung, he did as a teetotaling baseball executive once did, according to Casey Stengel, by hiring anyone who drank as long as he could slide across home plate. Lombardi couldn't or wouldn't grasp the fact that neither genius nor the new morality precluded the dedication necessary to bring success. When they put on the pads, Joe Namath, Paul Hornung and The NFL 4 did what they had to do to win.

The truth is that professional football has as much relevance outside its insular world as the UCLA pompom girls. It's a game, a terrific game, great entertainment. But its symbolism is anathema to the young. Hating opponents (Lombardi: "There's nothing that stokes fire like hate") and winning at all costs is neither a biblical nor a constitutional injunction. Respect and authority have to be earned in the outside world, not enforced by lifetime-binding contracts. It is not news that it takes hard work to achieve things, except possibly to the many jocks whose idea of work away from the football field is to get paid to let people look at them at store openings and banquets.

Lombardi's understanding that "it's a function

of the young" to try to change their world, cited earlier, was buried beneath the tough exterior of his tougher words. And *those* words, dangerously, have been picked up by every little high school despot with a whistle and a ball. How many of them will turn out kids with stories like Joseph Lombardi's in Jerry Kramer's, *Lombardi, Winning Is the Only Thing.*

> When I graduated from St. Cecilia's, I was all set to go to Fordham. And then they named Vin freshman coach, and I decided I'd had enough of playing for my brother. I went to St. Bonaventure, played football there as a freshman, then transferred to Fordham. As soon as I transferred, Fordham made Vince an assistant coach for the varsity. That did it for me. I switched back to St. Bonaventure, and then, when the Bonnies gave up football, I did too.

In professional football Vince Lombardi's hard credo did have relevance. With it, he won and he showed what it takes to keep winning.

"To Lombardi," said Henry Jordan, the tackle, "happiness was only one thing: lying exhausted in victory."

Lombardi was a winner because he was smarter than most of his competition, because he was an unyielding perfectionist and because he imposed his will on his players with the sheer force of his personality. He had some pretty good players too.

Presumably because it would be bad for his image, Lombardi was not esteemed as highly for his intellectual qualities as for his growling temper and demanding standards. There are thousands of coaches who growl; growling did not make Lombardi a great coach. There are thousands of coaches who are disciplinarians and physical fitness maniacs and they are pale imitations of him. Where Vince Lombardi beat them was in the brains department. (He graduated from Fordham with honors and taught Latin, math and science in high school.) When Lombardi went to Washington, Sonny Jurgensen said he learned more from him in a few hours than he had learned in twelve years as a pro. Bart Starr said: "The heart of his system was preparation. . . . That—more than words of encouragement he occasionally gave me—was what built up my self-confidence." The notion that all pro coaches know the Xs and Os of football as well as each other is as crazy as most football notions. There is no reason why one coach can't be better with Xs and Os than the next, any more than one mathematician can't be better than the next with numbers.

Lombardi's decision to build an offense around running was an intellectual as well as a visceral decision for him. It was the football he knew best. He grew up in an era when passing seemed as immoral as knee-high skirts. But he also sensed that you could run the ball in the NFL, contrary to the conventional wisdom that passing was the basic name of the game. He knew something the others didn't.

And he knew talent. In Green Bay, Lombardi walked into a backlog of top draft picks who hadn't been organized yet—Hornung, Taylor, Nitschke, Dowler, McGee, Gregg, Forrester, Currie, Jerry and Ron Kramer—and he picked up Thurston, Davis, Jordan and Quinlan in trades. He paired Hornung and Taylor in the backfield, and went to work on Starr. He inherited good players, he got more good players, he recognized ability in other players that could be adapted to his system. In his first few years he acquired Adderly, Jeter and Robinson in the draft. Those players were his nucleus for a decade. His first achievement with the Redskins was the discovery that rookie Larry Brown, who went on to lead the NFL in ground gaining last season, needed a hearing aid because he was late on the snap counts by a fraction of a second.

There was something beautifully old-fashioned yet bold in Lombardi's vision of how the game should and could be played. The boldness was in the pure personal risk of turning the clock back, in his first head coaching job since high school, at age forty-six. It was bold because his brand of football would make the highest demands on players in discipline. He would have to win and win fast because hard-driving martinets are tolerated only by winners.

The Packers did win fast. A winning season followed by a division title followed by the championship run. Football, like movies, is a director's medium and it doesn't take long for the good ones to put their stamp on a team. The Packers kept winning because of Lombardi's passion for perfection: his unwillingness to settle for an un-Packerlike performance in victory, his remorseless eye for the detail that revealed a softening of purpose. He pushed so hard to maintain his monument that late in his last season as coach in Green Bay he came to realize, like Hamlet, exactly what price he was paying. "I'm turning into an animal," he said.

Lombardi's boldness and hardness were manifest in one famous play that, typical of football, may have been a mistake. This was the last play of the 1967 championship game, from the 1-yard line. The Cowboys, who stressed finesse, tried to finesse themselves a touchdown in a similar situation in the 1966 championship game and wound up with the shouldas, couldas and wouldas. Now on the frozen tundra of their home field, with fifteen seconds and no timeouts left, trailing by three points, going for an unprecedented third straight championship, the Packers played fundamental you-and-me football—if we make it we win, if we don't you win—and Bart Starr scored on a quarterback sneak. Had he been stopped the clock would have run out before the field-goal unit, which was grouped on the sideline could swing into action. Lombardi, it developed, didn't know they wouldn't get another playoff if they failed. Standing in the Klondike cold of 13 below for three hours would numb anyone's mind.

Yet despite his reputation for unrelenting firmness and saintly ideals, Lombardi was flexible and pragmatic too. So if a heathen or a hell raiser could play football, and the Packers had their share of them, St. Vince didn't banish him to a retreat, he reveled in his redemption on the field. Soon after arriving in Green Bay, he found Ray Nitschke in an off-limits bar and swore he'd get rid of him, until his assistant coaches convinced him that they had no replacement; Lombardi relented by yielding to a vote of the players, who, with democracy suddenly thrust upon their shoulders, did their duty to God, family and team by voting unanimously to give Nitschke another chance. Lombardi traded long-time star Jim Ringo because he wanted to negotiate through an agent, but he gave Donny Anderson, an avowed swinger, a record $600,000 contract during the height of the AFL-NFL war. And when the juice in the powerhouse ground game began to dry up, Lombardi put the ball in the air and urged Starr to be reckless. And, of course, Lombardi was very flexible and pragmatic about himself when he left the Packers for the Redskins.

Stern patriarch that he was, Lombardi read

Jim Taylor out of the family when he played out his option to desert to the Saints, near his home in Louisiana, for a fat three-year contract at the end of his career. Ron Kramer had done the same several years before, going to the Lions. To Lombardi, Taylor's move was an act of disloyalty, against him and the Packers, in that order. So when Taylor and Paul Hornung were given a testimonial dinner in Green Bay—Hornung was jettisoned in an expansion draft, which was not an act of disloyalty apparently—Lombardi stayed away and sent a telegram quoting Cicero on loyalty. Taylor restrained himself from resending it when Lombardi deserted his duchy, jumping to the Redskins for 5 per cent of the action.

Lombardi's legendary temper, erupting from that volcanic-rock face, was an instrument that communicated fear, frustration, passion. Thus he became the big daddy and the players his children whose only desire was to please him—and shut him up. No player was safe from his scalding abuse. The available evidence suggests that many of them tuned him out and/or despised him for it. Lombardi often told them, "Without me you're nothing," which didn't endear him to them either; some of them replied privately that they wouldn't be able to stand him if they didn't win. He could bring tears to his eyes as deftly as Katharine Hepburn when he emoted about team love, but he rarely communicated love or respect to the players individually. He never told Jim Taylor, one of his greatest players, that he was even a good ballplayer. Taylor wanted to hear it from his lips. To Lombardi the team was Lombardi and Lombardi was the team.

Was the temper a mere expression of the necessary arrogance of a visionary, or was it a necessary tool too? Some psychologists have theorized that pep talks can have an hypnotic effect that expands horizons and capabilities. Others have demonstrated that their effects are temporary and perhaps illusionary, like greenies. "I work at the game all week," says Johnny Unitas. "I watch film and study and practice. That's my pep talk." Leave it at that. Only an old sourpuss would want to refute all the myths of locker room oratory.

Different strokes for different folks. Paul Brown and Weeb Ewbank, the two other most successful coaches of modern times, get results differently. Ewbank won two championships in Baltimore and one with the Jets—the only coach to build two pro championship teams from scratch—and he said at the 1969 Super Bowl that he didn't want his teams to froth at the mouth before a game, that he told dirty jokes to loosen them up if he suspected that they were. Maybe Dallas could have used some of that last January. The grandfatherly Ewbank is secure enough to let his players do their thing off the field as long as they do his thing on the field. He has a reputation among players for not being a zealot on physical conditioning, yet his teams seem to win more games in the last quarter than they lose. His secret? No secret. Organization and talent. "Put twelve guys in a room and have them jump over a ping-pong table," says Jimmy Orr, "and Ewbank can pick out the one who will be all-pro." He took the unknown Johnny Unitas off a sand lot and the well-known Joe Namath out of college and he knew what to do with them. He has a team now that could be a contender for years. And he is as cuddly as Lombardi was thorny.

Don McCafferty says, "If you treat players like men they'll perform like men. If they don't, get rid of them." Within the framework of football, this is how Ewbank, but not many others, operates too. Today's athlete generally is more mature and responsible than the storied ruffians of yesteryear and they are demanding adult treatment, but generally they are still treated like overgrown children. Paul Brown, as a card-carrying fuddy-duddy, shepherds his players en masse to movies the night before games but he doesn't let them get excited or corrupted by X-rated films.

Paul Brown revolutionized football, dragging it kicking and screaming into the second half of the twentieth century with modern business techniques, meticulous scouting and planning, play-by-play film breakdowns, innovations in strategy and tactics and on and on. He created the Cleveland Himselfs, who won eleven division and seven league championships in their first twelve seasons. He ruled with a ruthlessly fair business ethic, frowning on cheap sentiment and juvenile rah-rah. If a player did his job he was rewarded and if he didn't he became a former Himself. Brown didn't relate football to God's game plan or America's destiny; he was a coach trying to win games. He didn't lecture on love and hate; team goals and individual drive generated emotion naturally. But he ran the Himselfs with absolute, glacial, imperious authority and when he didn't win a championship for five years there was a rebellion, led by Jim Brown, and he was ousted. He has been more emotional but as sharp-tongued and biting as ever with the Cincinnati Bengals, who beat out the Himselfs to make the playoffs in their third year of existence. Motivation? In the seventh game of the season a safety man fell down on the job, permitting two touchdown passes. Next day he was gone. The Bengals then won seven in a row.

Brown has cool blood coursing through his veins, Lombardi had hot marinara sauce in his. Lombardi put everything in himself on the line and never let you forget it. When he died the media reacted as though he were our DeGaulle. "The finest example of leadership this country has known for some time," intoned Bart Starr, "was Vince Lombardi."

Football, we would learn, began with Vince Lombardi. Jerry Kramer credited him with such immortal homilies as: "Winning is not everything.

It is the only thing" (Hurry-Up Yost, 1905); and "Dancing is a contact sport. Football is a hitting sport" (Bob Zuppke, 1920s); and "You never lose. But sometimes the clock runs out on you" (Doak Walker on Bobby Layne, 1950s).

It is understandable. Vince Lombardi earned his players' respect and affection, for his religion was theirs. Winning.

THE MOVIE STAR

Vince Lombardi seldom was exposed to the public in a vulnerable position, when he wasn't in complete command of everything within a ten-mile radius. Perhaps the closest he came to it was during that 1967 NFL championship game, between the Packers and the Cowboys in the Icicle Bowl. Lombardi was barely visible under ridiculous layers of blankets, hats and snowshoes. The much-lionized lion looked meek and miserable. He couldn't command the weather.

On one semi-public occasion Lombardi was seen in a vulnerable position. Somebody else actually was his boss. He was doing a cameo bit for a movie.

The movie was George Plimpton's *Paper Lion*, and central casting came up with its most brilliant stroke since Pat O'Brien did Knute Rockne. They needed someone to play Vince Lombardi, and they got Vince Lombardi. Who else was there? Dustin Hoffman?

Lombardi arrived at a studio in New York at 9 A.M. and immediately let them know who he was. "As long as the lines are natural to a coach," he said, "everything will be all right." Which was his way of saying that these Hollywood types weren't going to give him a win-one-for-the-Gipper number. The movie's director, Alex March, grinned and began to explain the scene. Plimpton, played by Alan Alda, was to ask Lombardi if he could work out with the Packers to write a book about his experiences. Lombardi is supposed to be intrigued but he thinks Plimpton is some kind of nut and he turns him down, sweetly but firmly.

Now in real life Plimpton wouldn't have gotten into Lombardi's office in the first place, and if he had, Lombardi would have knocked him down with a shoulder block and said, "Turn in your uniform. We play to win." But on the set Lombardi thought the proposition was more fun than winning 60—0 and he kept smiling as the movie thing went on around him, props and cameras and workers moving about. "Look at him. He must be some taskmaster," one technician said, for even Lombardi's smile was ominous. "That's how you become a football coach. You beat everybody up."

The director called for a rehearsal and Lombardi went through his lines stiffly but without error. He was so pleased with himself that when he finished he cracked himself up and spun with glee. He was having fun and he was getting $3000 for the cameo role besides.

"Terrific," said the director. "Just one thing. Look him up and down. Look at those skinny legs . . ."

They were ready to roll. On the first take Alda blew a line. On the second take a camera blew a line. On the third take Lombardi blew a line and on the fourth he blew one again.

"You were reaching for words," the director said.

"I was? I wanted to say something," Lombardi said, his actor's discipline about to crack. "The more often we do this the more often I'm going to get hung up."

The director knew his man. "I'm the coach, Vinnie. We have to perfect one play at a time. Now, ready, on two, hut-hut."

"That's too rhythmic," Lombardi said, smiling his Boris Karloff smile again. "It's hut . . . hut . . ."

"Your ball, Vinnie."

Take five was perfect and Lombardi seemed to want to jump up and down and applaud himself. "I'm enjoying it," he said. "I'm enjoying it." But midway through the next scene he began to shake his head sourly. He was supposed to say, "But you see, Plimpton, we're carrying four quarterbacks. Asking a coach to carry five, that's tempting a coronary." He almost choked on the line.

"I'd never say that," he said. "Why don't I just say, 'Asking a coach to carry five, that's a real headache!'"

They did it that way, and it was fine, but there was trouble in the final scene, the exit scene with Lombardi showing Plimpton to the door. He was supposed to reach into his jacket and offer a cigar to Plimpton. It was awkward for Lombardi. "The truth of the matter," he said, "is that I don't smoke."

This created a momentary crisis. The director, the producer and several others huddled, searching for a new exit scene. After ten minutes Lombardi wandered over and said, "How about this— I say to him as he leaves, 'Have you tried the AFL?'"

"Wait a minute, son," said the director. "Do I tell you how to coach? Terrific. Terrific."

"They'll love me in the AFL for this," Lombardi said. "I'm real big with the AFL."

They had to do it four times to get it right and Lombardi didn't mind at all. He guffawed after each take, an improvisational actor pleased with his sudden invention. "I'm a movie star," chortled Vince Lombardi.

7. THE SENSUOUS QUARTERBACK

Sigmund Freud of the unbeaten Vienna Libidos was named coach of the year in the NFL today.

"The whole secret to coaching professional football is sex," Freud said. "There isn't much difference physically in the teams in this league. The big difference is sexually. We think we can beat any team on any given Saturday night, and when we do, look out for us on Sunday."

Freud said he stressed two fundamentals: bedcheck and individual pep talks, which he called psychoanalysis.

"In psychoanalysis we try to build the aggressive sexual drive that football players must have," Freud said. "I call it psychosexual development. If your libido isn't in shape, if you haven't resolved your oedipal conflicts, you'll surrender in the fourth quarter. Sexual fatigue makes cowards of us all.

"Bedcheck, to us, is the practice field. This is where we prepare for our games. We check all beds at three A.M. If anyone is sleeping without a mate, it's an automatic hundred dollar fine. Teams don't go physically stale, they go sexually stale.

"Because of this system the best players in the league play out their options to join us. That is why we are unbeatable."

ACROSS the field he came in that ambling pool-room slouch. For much of America Joe Namath is the only man on the field when he is on a field, but this time he was alone literally, ambling toward a television interview through a valley of boos and hoots. It was half time at an exhibition game between the Jets and the Giants in the Yale Bowl, New Haven, Connecticut, and here came Joe Namath in violet bell bottoms—boo—white sockless loafers — hoot — a flowered shirt — boo-hoot—helmeted with a beautiful coiffeur—hoot-boo. He was, as always, one of the truly fantastic species of fauna ever to appear on a playing field. And, as always, he inspired catatonic fits among the multitudes the likes of which we haven't seen since Marat/Sade.

Joe Namath, threat to the moral order of the universe, is one of the most important athletes this country has ever spawned.

What foul deed had he done to arouse the natives this time? His annual summer caper. For the fourth straight summer Joe Namath had blasphemed, launching dialogues of righteous debate on his fitness to throw a football in polite society. Having made a movie with Ann Margret over the winter, a movie with much kissy-kissy and other bad stuff, he arrived weeks late for training. Since walking up stairs was torture for Namath's wrecked knees, they certainly could do with as little training as he could get away with. And exhibitions were a bloody bore anyway; he'd be twice the fool to risk his fool neck and knees in glorified scrimmages. (When he did, one season later, he suffered another knee injury in the first exhibition, shelving him for most of the season and launching a national dialogue on the foolishness of such charades.)

But he was Joe Namath and so his absence had become an international incident. A teammate, linebacker Al Atkinson, made a delayed appearance too, after threatening retirement, partially, he said, because he'd like to see his quarterback grow up. Laid bare for the fans was another rare view into the body politic of a football team, sliced open by a quarterback who defied every holy-holy about the game.

There is an undercurrent of tribalism on every team, based on race, position, salary, geography, life style, and so on. It rarely is harmful, it seldom comes to the surface, and winning usually keeps it submerged. But the pros and cons of Namath, who had led the Jets to a championship and

a division title in the previous two seasons, polarized his teammates. Predictably, with a couple of
exceptions, they were split along offensive and defensive lines (although most players liked him
personally). One notable exception was Matt
Snell, the fullback, who made no secret of his
contempt for what he saw as a double standard in
the organization's indulgence of Namath. Yet
nobody blocked harder or more efficiently for
Namath than Snell: that was his job.

Actually there was little the organization could
do about Namath except hand him the ball and
say, "Play nice," as the Lions did with Bobby
Layne, who raised hell in his day, and as many
teams have done with many superstars. But the
flap over Namath and Atkinson was totally incomprehensible to fans who had been brainwashed to
believe that ball teams, especially football teams,
are love machines. Unless they play in Green
Bay and can't avoid bumping into each other in
the street, some players might not talk to each
other for years simply because they play on separate units, practice on separate ends of the field,
attend separate meetings, live in separate worlds.
Maybe that's what the pre-game prayer is all
about, a way to introduce the players to each
other.

Said Dave Herman, offensive guard, about the
anguished cries of dissension rising once more
from the ashes of yesterday's newspapers: "When

Joe came back I felt like throwing a bouquet of roses to him. He'll be there when we need him."

Joe Namath played four games of football before he suffered a wrist injury and was sidelined for the duration of that 1970 season, a season that then needed the heroics of George Blanda, a forty-three-year-old quarterback, and Tom Dempsey, a no-toed place kicker who kicked a 63-yard field goal, to rescue it from a severe depression in drama. Still, America's most admired writer, its most controversial public servant and its most Olympian political columnist dramatized the importance of being Joe Namath.

Norman Mailer on the National Aeronautics and Space Administration's antiseptic promotional approach to moonshots: "Unless they get someone like Joe Namath as an astronaut, they're in terrible trouble," because the public will lose interest.

J. Edgar Hoover: "You won't find long hair or sideburns à la Joe Namath here. There are no hippies in the FBI. The public has an image of what an agent should look like."

James Reston: "Joe Namath is not only in tune with the rebellious attitude of the young, but he doubles it. He defies both the people who hate playboys and the people who hate bullyboys. He is something special: a long-haired hard-hat, the anti-hero of the sports world."

You have to go back to Babe Ruth to find an athlete who had the impact on his game that Namath has. Ruth brought baseball back after the Black Sox Scandal by swinging a bat with theatrical gusto. Namath changed the face of professional football with one orgasmic victory, in the 1969 Super Bowl. Ruth's spats with management were every bit as controversial as Namath's. But Ruth kept his Ruthian boozing and wenching private, and his historic "bellyache" had been identified by some historians as a social disease. The importance of Joe Namath is that there is very little about him that is private.

Bursting on the scene in the age of television, in a hot game, football, and at a time of social upheaval, especially among the young, Namath's impact as old-fashioned *bon vivant* and new-fashioned iconoclast is staggering.

He liberated the athlete from the centuries-old chastity belt of false morality. The athlete doesn't have to list his sexual conquests on the statistical charts, as Namath does, but neither is he compelled any more to present himself as a defender of the faith and neatest of tricks—virile eunuch. He can even cry real tears as Namath did in public when he said he was quitting football because he had been ordered by Pete Rozelle to get rid of his bar.

The immediate visible result was that athletes like Johnny Bench and Derek Sanderson began showing up on television as pleasantly hip flip young men, the new breed of jock, personable entertainers rather than neuter bullet heads. (Although Jack Concannon of the Bears complained, "They want us to play like Joe Namath, but we can't look like him.") Fran Tarkenton observed that it was possible for an athlete to take a drink in public now without being accused of getting roaring drunk. Son of a Georgia preacher, Tarkenton said Namath had broken through his stereotyped ideas about people. Looks and life styles, Tarkenton decided, could be deceiving. He understood better than most that it took more than pure talent to play football the way Joe Namath does.

That message might be trickling out to America subliminally. Meanwhile the fallout from Namath's white-shoes-long-hair-anti-Establishment image was upsetting many parents because it created serious problems in selling athletes as plastic heroes. This was a good thing but the parents didn't think so. Wrote Pete Axthelm in *Newsweek*, in a piece on a heralded rookie quarterback: "Terry Bradshaw looms not only as a potential superstar, but also as a knight-errant of sport, destined to somehow guide the youth of America away from Namath's swinging broads and bars and into a promised land of the clean-cut and the fair." But it's never going to happen again, because the youth simply will defect to the next sonic-boom rock group or whatever, as they may have been about to do when Namath proved to be one of their own.

Finally Namath influenced the uneasy truce

between uptight high school and college coaches and their players. The coaches thought the kids were going to hell in a communal bus because they were showing dangerous signs of being part of their generation. With Namath proving their point, players have gotten some concessions in being treated more like real students, i.e., people. They still have a long way to go before coaches concede that their authority isn't challenged by a mustache but total alienation has been averted. (A sociologist at UCLA took a survey that showed there were fewer candidates for football in Los Angeles high schools because the kid who plays the guitar and has a social conscience has as much status among his peers as a kid who plays tackle. Drops in turnouts for high school teams have been reported in other cities. It is something for the coaches to think about.)

Elinor Kaine inadvertently took her own sociological survey on Joe Namath. Possessed of one Joe Namath white shoe, given to her by a Jet equipment man, she offered it as a prize to her readers in a letter-writing contest. She got a nationwide response from girls who thought it would be better than a glass slipper, from boys who thought it would transform them into passing demons. An entire class in a grade school in Des Moines, Iowa, entered the contest; there's a teacher out there with his or her finger on the pulse of America.

The idea of little boys and girls hero-worship-ping Joe Namath was enough to make William Buckley's eyebrows quiver with fear for the decline of Western civilization. For behind much of the paranoia about Namath were clearly defined moral imperatives. Not only did he seem to defy conventions of hard work and team play ethics, but he made the titillating confession that he was an all-pro at sexual fore and post game play. He was quoted in *Playboy* magazine to the effect that he left the Catholic church because he didn't see anything wrong with sex. He checked his trophy room and counted three hundred pubic scalps. He put his name to a boorish bump-and-run autobiography that might have been titled "The Sensuous Quarterback." Inexplicably he failed to reveal whether his quick release was a condition of all his bodily functions, or just of his arm.

Joe Namath's Beaver Falls Imperative hasn't won any popularity contests with women's liberationists—"You've heard the old saying about there being a boy for every girl in the world?" said comedian Flip Wilson of Namath. "Well, here's the boy they meant."—but his candor stripped away the last of the jock taboos. Bud Wilkinson once expressed the moral imperative of athletes this way: "Drinking a beer won't hurt a player physically. But it is a chink in his moral armor." But that implies guilt, and there is no guilt if it doesn't violate a personal code of ethics.

There are jocks who could have carnal knowledge of baby sea otters and sleep the sleep of the pure.

Larry Grantham, a teammate of Namath's, said he hardly knew there was an opposite sex until he went to college, so wrapped up in football was he in his small town Mississippi high school. Coaches, as guardians of sex-is-evil morality, used to warn that sex ("Sleep with your hands over the blankets") could steal your energy in the night. What they really were concerned about was that sex, or love, especially love, would divert athletes from the monastic dedication they think is required to score touchdowns. Few if any jocks pay attention to such nonsense in college and none in the pros, for they discovered long before psychologists did that sex is not harmful physiologically and that sex and games are mutually compatible parts of the same world of intense experience.

Weeb Ewbank put the matter in professional perspective when an assistant coach told him that the Jets were being seduced by college girls at their training site. "That's one good thing about this place," Ewbank said. "They don't have to go driving to New York at all hours for it.

But nobody throws touchdown passes every Sunday or scores every Sunday night, and that goes for Joe Namath too. A movie actress with a weakness for quarterbacks, and linebackers, pitchers, forwards, goalies and the rest of the menagerie, tells a touching story. On her first date with a famous unmarried quarterback, at an all-star game, he put her up in a suite in a hotel. But she was stricken by a sudden case of virtue and informed him that he would have to return to his hotel and try again on second down. She retired to her bedroom, only to find, hours later, the quarterback asleep on a couch outside her door. "Get out," she cried. "You're just trying to make those guys think you're sleeping with me." He slinked out, defeated. Football is a game of adversity.

The first hint anyone had that Joe Namath was going to stand astride the land like the Colossus of Rhodes came in 1967, just before his third season. Although the Jets hadn't had a winning season with him, he had already guaranteed the success of the team and the AFL. He did this with an electrifying performance in his last college game, in the Orange Bowl. Sonny Werblin, president of the Jets and a prominent executive in show business, said it was the greatest pilot (test) film he ever saw, and he signed Namath to the celebrated $400,000 contract. Presto: the Jets sold thirty thousand season tickets, the AFL secured its beachhead in New York, television ratings climbed and the merger with the NFL was ordained. The Jets, purchased by Werblin and friends for less than a million dollars in 1963, are valued today at about $20 million.

Now, in the summer of 1967, Namath walked out of preseason camp because, he said, of personal problems. He spent a night on the town in New York, got into a scuffle with a sportswriter, was fined $500 by the Jets—and made headlines all over the country for three days. He had arrived.

After a winning season, Namath caused another furor the next summer when he missed several exhibitions due to a salary dispute. A sportswriter for the *New York Times* recommended that the Jets trade him because a team couldn't win with a selfish player like that. It was the funniest story of the year until Tex Maule wrote in *Sports Illustrated* just before the Super Bowl four months later: "Most experts, for unfathomable reasons, have conceded the Jets an edge at quarterback."

There has never been a season quite like 1968 or a game quite like the 1969 Super Bowl for a football player, one twenty-five-year-old presence confronting the country with its moral hangups. Namath grew a Fu Manchu mustache, then a stylish rage, and a dozen Jets followed suit. Milt Woodward, commissioner of the AFL, wrote them a letter saying it was bad for football's image to be identified with extremist elements in society. Joe Namath said that Milt Woodward could tell everyone how extremely brutal and savage football is if he seeks the truth. Someone stuffed a packet of religious literature into Namath's locker; Namath stuffed it back in the donor's hand and said, wrong pew. A black player said Namath was responsible for the racial harmony on the team, because of his unaffected color-blindness. Namath said, "I stink," after he threw five interceptions in a game. And the Jets didn't lose for another year.

Before the heavyweight championship fight between Muhammad Ali and Joe Frazier in March, 1970, comedian Bill Cosby said, "I'm so excited I wish they'd fight a whole week." Joe Namath had that kind of week at the Super Bowl.

Joe Namath is no hippie but in January 1969 a young person who questioned authority, religion and society's hypocrisy, and who didn't take a haircut every three weeks, was automatically hooked up with Alan Ginsberg, Haight-Ashbury and dirty feet. Namath drove a Lincoln, lived in a penthouse, was a devout hedonist, affected Frank Sinatra's glass-in-hand insouciance, and would rather go one-on-one with Dick Butkus than sit in the mud for three days at Woodstock to listen to rock music. But America saw him as a hippie—there was no doubt in anyone's mind that if he were a girl he wouldn't wear a brassiere —and that was that. He was ranked alongside the Beatles, Bobby Dylan and Muhammad Ali as symbols of a decade's decadence.

Flying to Miami Namath began a week-long assault on all the time-honored traditions of pre-game conduct. He remarked that there were four or five quarterbacks in the AFL superior to Earl Morrall, who was the most valuable player in the NFL. Since Namath obviously was one of the four or five, the interpretation given this candid and accurate appraisal of the talent in the room was that Namath was saying he was better than Morrall. A no-no.

Namath was cast in the role of the villain from that moment on, stealing the role from teammate Johnny Sample, who came by it naturally and eagerly and, what's more, was a former Colt. When Namath failed to show up at a photographer's session the first day in Miami, noting that 10 A.M. was an indecent hour for a civilized man to get up, it was taken as further evidence of his lack of team spirit and disrespect for authority. A second no-no.

When he made headlines after a night-club debate with Lou Michaels of the Colts, insisting the Jets would win, it was feared that Namath had a death wish. Third no-no.

This was followed by his famous "guarantee" that the Jets would win, given at a banquet, and that no-no convinced wizened NFL heads that he should be muzzled for his own safety because he was giving the Colts so much ammunition—newspaper clippings—that they would break his legs like uncooked spaghetti. The Colts started as seventeen-point favorites and gained so much support that the spread soared to nineteen and higher by game time.

What happened on that Sunday, January 12, 1969, was best described by George Sauer, who caught ten passes from Namath. It was, said Sauer, like the day Copernicus told earthlings that the sun didn't rotate around them. "It must have been fantastic to find out you weren't the center of the universe," he said.

For three hours 75 million viewers on television saw the end of the world as they knew it. And it blew minds. They had been convinced that the AFL was a planet to the NFL's sun. They had been convinced by the pro football mystique that a quarterback had to be Bart Starr or Johnny Unitas to win championships, leading by example, modesty, discipline, character and attendance at communion breakfasts. The quarterback was the new American ideal of sound mind and body. Joe Namath might be able to throw a football, but his mind was scattered and his body vulnerable. For the fans who bought that theology whole, it was a three-hour horror show. Attacking a defense that had set NFL records, Namath ran the game as resourcefully as Starr and threw lightning bolts like Unitas. The Jets won 16–7. The next day this "Owed to Joe Willie," written by Jim Dance, appeared on the editorial page of the *Miami Herald:*

> Somebody said it couldn't be done but he with a chuckle replied take the 17 points and bet your grandma's Social Security if need be because there ain't no way for us to lose to them Colts.
>
> Dolts.
>
> Here and there he is known as Broadway Joe for commercial reasons because of a ham-

burger chain of the same name although it is not likely he would be caught dead on Broadway near The Times or Ochses.

Preferring Foxes.

He is a cat who not only can do it but he will tell you he can and then intimate how and when and in what manner and means and then he will just go ahead and do it, as much as some may

Rue it.

Audacity thy name is Joe Willie and you come along in a pussyfoot era when everybody else is saying we will do our best and hope for the rest and that's the way the ball bounces when they lose.

But not youse.

THE MESSIAH

Roman Gabriel says he has to know 180 plays to audible to at the line of scrimmage. Murray Kempton says nobody knows 180 of anything. So how does a quarterback do what he has to do?

One day Al Davis watched the Jets play his Raiders and every time the Raiders shifted into a new defense Joe Namath audibled to a new play. Davis, knowing the soft spots in the particular defense, would say Namath was going to do this now, and Namath would do that, hitting the soft spot.

Then somebody hit Namath, very hard, and he

got up very slowly. "Now let's see what the sonof-abitch does," Davis said.

"He usually gets up and throws a touchdown pass," someone said.

"We'll see," said Davis.

He saw. Namath threw a touchdown pass of some 60 yards on the next play, arrowing one of those deep-line drives that make football people gasp.

In the Super Bowl Namath beat the Baltimore blitz, which had terrorized NFL opponents, by throwing to George Sauer on prearranged routes. Namath read defenses and Sauer read Camus and they communicated perfectly.

"With two great athletes," said Weeb Ewbank, reducing the game to its basic components, "it works."

The quarterback as Messiah can do these things, but he earns his M only if he wins. That is what quarterbacking is about and that's why the quickest way to the top is to get a quarterback who is so good he compensates for other weaknesses on a team. It is also the best guarantee for a team without significant weaknesses to win championships. The top three picks in the 1971 draft and two of the top three in 1970 were quarterbacks. The value of stock in the Patriots increased by a million and a half dollars the day after they earned the right to draft Jim Plunkett of Stanford by finishing with the poorest record in pro football last season.

If Plunkett becomes a Messiah—and he gave every indication that he may—he will be one of the rare ones. You can count how many there have been on your fingers, and if you've misplaced a couple thumbs, you would still have enough.

There have been eight great quarterbacks: Baugh (a tailback but essentially a passer), Luckman, Waterfield, Graham, Van Brocklin, Layne, Unitas, Starr. They have one thing in common: they each won at least two championships. Defining their value, the Rams and Eagles haven't won championships since Van Brocklin left them, the Redskins and Lions haven't won championships since Baugh and Layne retired, the Bears and Browns have won just one championship apiece since Luckman and Graham retired, the Colts have never won a championship without Unitas. In the vernacular of Hollywood, they weren't chopped liver.

Starr started out as a mechanic who was carried by a great team, the Packers, and he developed into a quarterback who carried the team on to more championships as it began to wear down. Mechanics usually remain mechanics but with the right team they can win championships too. Billy Wade with the Bears of 1963, Frank Ryan with the Browns of 1964, Len Dawson with the Chiefs of 1969 are three recent examples. If the Dallas Cowboys had a mechanic—a solid workmanlike quarterback who wouldn't lose games rather than a quarterback who wins them with virtuoso performances—they probably would have won their first championship by now.

The quarterbacks mentioned here come in all sizes and shapes, personalities and temperaments, but not colors. Black players have disproved all the old stereotypes—"They don't have the guts" has evolved to "Nothing hurts them"—but there have been no regular black pro quarterbacks. It is simplistic to confine the blame for this to pathological racism in the NFL. Black quarterbacks have been getting opportunities in recent years. The Raiders drafted one on the first round three years ago; he didn't make it. The Colts drafted a black quarterback on the third round this year. The Bills have a black backup quarterback.

There are reasons. The percentage of college quarterbacks who make it in the pros is minuscule. The percentage of black quarterbacks in college is minuscule. That stacks the percentages heavily against them, starting with the cycle of poorer coaching, poorer facilities and poorer competition in black high schools, which affects quarterback, as a memory bank position, more than other positions. Jimmy Jones of Southern Cal is the first black pro-type passing quarterback to play first string for three years on a major college team.

There was a time when the pros wouldn't accept a black quarterback. That time is past. A black Messiah is coming.

8. TALE OF
TWO CITIES

Under a gray October sky on the Plains of Troy yesterday the mighty defense of the Trojans made their last goal-line stand. A trick play by the Greeks pushed over the winning score in the dying minutes.

Odysseus, the quarterback for the invaders, said that after slamming into a stone wall for ten years he decided to use the old Wooden Horse play. "They have the best front four in the league," Odysseus said. "We felt we could distract them by spreading our ends and halfbacks. I just galloped alone up the middle. Normally I run only from sheer fright."

The victory of the Greeks stilled rumors of dissension and an impending coaching change because they hadn't scored in such a long time. It had been reported that Achilles, the great defensive end, was feuding with Agamemnon, the head coach. Agamemnon admitted that some players were unhappy, but he said it was a healthy sign.

He was more concerned with the crippling heel injury suffered by Achilles. It may end his career. Achilles said he was hit from behind by Paris. "It was a cheap shot," he said.

WITH apologies to that great English scribe, Charles Dickens, this is a tale of two cities that have known the best and the worst of times in professional football, Philadelphia and New York. In the decade of the NFL's greatest growth, the '60s, the Philadelphia Eagles and the New York Giants had the best of times immediately followed by the worst, bringing to the surface the supreme nuttiness that is one of homo sap's enduring charms.

First some background music.

The Eagles and the Giants are two of the seven pioneer franchises in the modern NFL dating from 1933. The others are the Pittsburgh Steelers, the Green Bay Packers, the Washington (nee Boston) Redskins, the Chicago Bears and the St. Louis (nee Chicago) Cardinals.

Four pioneer families still run their teams: the Maras of the Giants, the Bidwells of the Cardinals, the Rooneys of the Steelers, the Halases of the Bears. George Preston Marshall founded the

Redskins, Bert Bell the Eagles, Curley Lambeau the Packers. Tim Mara, Charles Bidwell and Art Rooney were self-made sportsmen about town associated with horse racing. George Halas, Bell and Lambeau were player-coach-entrepreneurs. Marshall was a promoter.

Halas is the crusty patriarch of pro football. He brought it off the sand lots when he signed Red Grange out of Illinois, and he built a dynasty with Bronco Nagurski, Bulldog Turner, Sid Luckman, George McAfee and others. Undaunted by winning just one of the six championships in the last twenty-five years, he still uses his prerogative as owner to send in plays now and then.

That is one, or six, more championships than the Steelers have won though. The Steelers do not even have a division title to their name. Unfortunately Art Rooney, one of the beautiful people of sports, squeezed most of his luck into a legendary three-day spree in the '30s when he won about $250,000 at the track. He had Johnny Unitas and Sid Luckman, and neither played a game for him before they were traded. He also once ran for a minor political office on the platform that he didn't know what the duties were but he would find out if elected; the *New York Times* hailed him as a Diogenes but he was defeated.

The Cardinals won their only championship in 1947. Jimmy Conzleman, coach of that team, is in the legend class too. In addition to playing and coaching and briefly owning a team, he wrote songs, published a newspaper, boxed, was a radio commentator and an advertising executive. Supreme Court Justice William O. Douglas spoke in his behalf when he was inducted into the Hall of Fame.

Curley Lambeau talked a packing house into investing $500 in the Packers in 1919, the year the old original NFL began. They won three championships in the early days, three more with Don Hutson and five with Lombardi. Today the Packers are publicly owned by fans who bought stock to keep them in Green Bay.

George Preston Marshall was bombastic, innovative and self-destructively bigoted. Two out of three ain't bad, but the third spoiled a good thing and Washington teams for a long time. Marshall conceived rules changes that opened up the game—most notably permitting passing anywhere behind the line of scrimmage (instead of at least five yards behind it) and slimming down the ball so it could be passed easily—and then he got Sammy Baugh. Pretty good thinking, and the Redskins won their two championships with it, the last in 1942. But Marshall's refusal to sign a black player until 1962 led to a decline and fall that hasn't become a rise and climb yet.

With Halas and Marshall, Bert Bell was a third dynamic force in the growth of the NFL. Remembered now primarily as a strong commissioner who made the home-television blackout policy stick in the courts, it was Bell who conceived the player draft in 1936. Unbeknownst to him, it would mark a prenatal reference for the schizophrenia of the Eagles. The first collegian drafted in the first draft was Jay Berwanger, an All-American halfback from the University of Chicago. The Eagles drafted him and he was stillborn, refusing to go pro. A prophetic development. Or, as Casey Stengel would say, the future of the Eagles was ahead of them.

The Eagles won championships in 1948 and 1949, with Greasy Neale coaching players like Steve Van Buren, Chuck Bednarik and Pete Pihos. A syndicate of a hundred businessmen put up $3000 apiece to buy the team, and in 1950 the head of the syndicate, a powerful politician, reamed out the players like so many ward heelers after a losing game. Neale told him to get out of his dressing room, and the politician fired him when the season was over. Nothing failed like success or succeeded like failure for the Eagles, as events would continue to prove.

In 1958 they got Norm Van Brocklin from the Rams in a trade. With Bob Waterfield and ends Tom Fears and Elroy Hirsch, Van Brocklin had helped make the Rams a devastating offensive team. In one game he passed for 550 yards, in another he threw five touchdown passes in one quarter. He would become the only quarterback to win championships in two cities and the only player in modern times to a) retire after being named the most valuable player in the league, and b) get a job as a head coach right after retiring. He was special.

When the Eagles did poorly in his first season playing with them, Van Brocklin decided they were a dead end and he wasn't going to die with them and, at age thirty-three, he would quit. The Eagles changed his mind with the promise, suggested by Commissioner Bell, that he would be named coach after the next season. The Eagles tied for second place that next season, but Bell died and the Eagles told Van Brocklin that coach Buck Shaw would like to take one last shot at a championship. Van Brocklin went along with it.

The Eagles then won the championship in 1960 as Van Brocklin had what many of his peers consider the one best season a quarterback ever had. And they don't know the half of it. What Van Brocklin did for all to see was win eight games in the last quarter and then beat the Packers in the playoff—nobody did that again to a Lombardi team—with a collection of culls, castoffs, old pros and a few young lions. What they didn't see was Van Brocklin being consulted by management on key trades, Van Brocklin tutoring backs Tommy McDonald and Pete Retzlaff as they converted to all-pro receivers, Van Brocklin virtually coaching the offense, Van Brocklin walking on the Schuylkill River.

With his soles still wet, Van Brocklin was asked by the Eagles what he wanted as head coach. He said he wanted to name his assistants, which is standard procedure, and that the organization should upgrade its college scouting system by investing $50,000 in it. They said no, and they said no. The first no was all Van Brocklin had to hear. It meant they were reneging on their promise. It meant he was as dead as Bell as far as they were concerned. He took the head coaching job with the brand new Minnesota Vikings.

Van Brocklin had perceived that pro football was changing and that the Eagles weren't changing with it. You could see the change at the draft meetings that were held then in Philadelphia. Cleveland's Paul Brown, who had revolutionized the game with total organization and intensive scouting, would be seated at a table laden with fat notebooks and fatter files and telephones, surrounded by seven or eight assistants. They might have been planning the production of Chevrolets for five years. The Eagles' table would have a half-filled three-by-five-inch card file as a centerpiece, period. It would be surrounded by a general manager and one assistant; their only scout might be out calling on a public telephone. They might have been bill collectors. Like as not, the president of the team, who was the fire commissioner of Philadelphia, would mosey over to the table, finger the three-by-five-inch cards, fish one out and say, "Here's a kid from Idaho, 6-5 and 245. Why don't we try him?"

There was a certain down-home logic to drafting from the Look All-America in those days, even if it was like fighting General Motors with a covered wagon. Until 1960, when expansion and the AFL intruded on the established order, there was a surplus of talent. Such a surplus that you might get a Van Brocklin in a trade and win a championship that way once in a great while, so why go to all the expense of a college scouting network? The Browns collected so many studs that they traded away Doug Atkins and Henry Jordan. The Rams, first of the older NFL teams to go heavily into scouting college talent, gave Andy Robustelli and Del Shofner to the Giants. All-pros all.

The danger in the practice of depending on rejects and trades was in the delusion that it could go on forever. Then, when it became necessary to compete with organization and cash for talent, the pioneer owners who had been paying linemen a couple hundred dollars a game twenty years before simply couldn't bring themselves to do it, despite soaring income from attendance and television. The Baltimore Colts, one of the more enlightened franchises, won championships in 1958 and 1959, were making an estimated million-dollar profit a year, and lost their No. 1 pick in 1960 to the AFL because they offered him $8500: he was Ron Mix, who became an all-AFL tackle for ten years. The Eagles didn't sign a No. 1 for the first four years of the war with the AFL, leading both leagues.

The penury of the Eagles inspired the first serious incident in labor-management relations in the NFL, known in labor history as The Great Quarterback Sneak of 1963. Ten days before the first game of the season, Sonny Jurgensen and King Hill left camp because management, as was its custom, negotiated by not negotiating; if a player didn't like the terms offered him he could wait until he did like them. While Jurgensen and Hill were condemned by managements and apologists from coast to coast for leaving their teammates in the lurch, the fact was that their teammates celebrated them as their Debs and Gompers. They gave them a roaring send-off when they departed and two days later, after their demands were met, they gave them heroes' welcomes.

At the end of that season the Eagles were sold for five and a half million dollars, netting a $52,-000 profit per share in fourteen years. Had the stockholders waited two months they could have made another $20,000 or so per share because of a $400,000-per-team raise in the league's television contract. Had they waited until 1968 they could have made $160,000 per share, because the team was then sold for $16 million and change.

Between sales there were five seasons of Katzenjammer madness. The new owner after the 1963 season was Jerry Wollman, a construction tycoon whose net worth, according to an NFL investigation, was $25 million. His choice as coach was

Joe Kuharich, who turned out to be the costliest football dummy in the annals of block and tackle.

Jerry Wollman, thirty-seven, bright and ebullient, had bought himself the ultimate toy and he was going to have some fun with it. He did, while the money lasted. He spent money like he had terminal cancer. He gave a Rolls-Royce to a stockholder who showed him around town to set up the purchase of the team. He took a gang of friends and relatives to Puerto Rico for a few weeks. He paid the mortgages of some assistant coaches. He rented a fire engine to pick up friends for a party. He bought Connie Mack Stadium. He picked up an expansion hockey franchise and financed a 15,000-seat arena. He was a flamboyant doer and he was jolting Philadelphia out of its conservative sloth.

But he screwed up the Eagles worse than they had been, which was no small achievement. He started by giving Joe Kuharich the gaudiest contract the mind of man could imagine—fifteen years at about $50,000 per. "I never made a mistake," Wollman replied.

In two years a building he was putting up in Chicago began to sink into Lake Michigan and he began to go down with it. He brought an Arabian sheik to one game, and a German prince to another, trying to arrange loans that would salvage his construction empire, his struggling team and his strange coach. He couldn't. Money was tight. He was declared bankrupt and ordered to put the team on the market. Every once in awhile a wind would blow off the roof of his arena, the Spectrum, which he had to sell too, to remind people of his whirlwind fate.

The inescapable conclusion about this bizarre period was the Joe Kuharich magic had done the job again. His record preceded him to Philadelphia: he had been the only losing coach in Notre Dame history, he had coached six years in the NFL (five with the Redskins, one with the Cardinals) and he had had one winner. He had always inherited losing situations and had always been equal to them. Wollman's infatuation with him seemed hypnotic. Perhaps it was explained by the time he caught a pass in practice and Kuharich told him he would have been a hotdamn flanker.

Kuharich went to work on the team and the fans soon after he took over. He traded Tommy McDonald, the wonderful little end, and Sonny Jurgensen, who had backed up Van Brocklin. There's nothing wrong with trading stars to build a better mousetrap or end run or defense, but a pattern began to emerge from those early moves that suggested self-destructive impulses. In return for McDonald the Eagles got Sam Baker, a kicker, and two ruptured steers, for Jurgensen they got Norm Snead. Kuharich went on to turn star halfback Tim Brown into a jangle of confusion, force the premature retirement of Pete Retzlaff and trade off four more solid players for about a thousand yards of ace bandages. And in an especially acute fit of paranoia he fired his public relations director because he couldn't control criticism of him in the press.

Another pattern emerged. Whatever his talent for doodling with Xs and Os, Kuharich had a lot of trouble when they became people. He couldn't or wouldn't communicate. Asked once what Kuharich said to him after an hour-long meeting, Sonny Jurgensen replied, "You've talked to him. Who knows?" After Jerry Wollman saw the double-talk comedian Al Kelly perform at a banquet, he shook his head and said, "He sounded like my coach."

Kuharich spoke a private tongue made up of equal parts evasion, malaprop, Stengelese and crooked thinking. These are some of his classics:

"The charge on that blocked kick came either from the inside or the outside."

"Trading quarterbacks is rare but not unusual."

"I'm not vacillating you. I can only answer a question about a conclusive."

"We were three points behind, but that's not the same as being even."

"A missed block here, a missed assignment there, it adds up [after a 56—7 defeat]."

The farewell season of Kuharich and Wollman proved to be a dramatic tour de force. They showed that losing wasn't everything, it was the only thing. The Eagles lost their first ten games. "They say you can't win them all," said Kuharich.

"I say sometimes you can't win one." But with perfection in his grasp—and with the fabulous O. J. (Orange Juice) Simpson theirs in the draft for the losing—they won their next two games and blew it. Kuharich refined the art of losing to its finite limit—losing while winning.

The NFL remains heavily in debt to him for that because it created a comic theater of the absurd. Fans today watch the anti-heroes on the bottom with almost as much zeal as they watch the heroes on top. The race for the poorest record in the league and thus the top draft choice is a game-within-the-game that can be more fun than all the other names of the game, like watching film run backward. The Eagles played the Steelers in what was called the Orange Juice Bowl in 1968, and it was a classic. The score was 3—3 going into the last minute, the teams as futile as the law allows. Then Kuharich ordered the Eagles to try for a first down on fourth down from their own 10-yard line. No dummy he. The Steelers held, kicked a field goal to win and the nation cheered the winless Eagles wildly.

By that time people were even cheering in Philadelphia. A group of fans tried to organize a boycott to demonstrate their disgust over what they branded a civic disgrace, but it was doomed. Philadelphia fans had long been conditioned to watching games out of morbid curiosity. Besides, the sale of the Eagles was assured, to trucking magnate Len Tose, who had already promised to fire Kuharich as his first official act. The goofy saga of Jerry Wollman and Joe Kuharich came to an end with the fans still cheering, disproving the canard, first uttered by Bo Belinsky, that Philadelphians boo funerals.

Kuharich had one winning season in five with the Eagles, giving him two winners in his last fifteen years as a head coach, and his contract does not expire until 1979. He left a mark they will be shooting at for a long time.

Until a few years ago, oddly coinciding with the Wollman-Kuharich capers, the Giants had never experienced such turbulence. They were one of the cornerstone franchises in the league, formed in 1925, winning a championship of the old NFL two years later and winning three championships and ten division titles after that. There were smooth transitions of both family front-office control and field leadership. Steve Owens, who had been an outstanding tackle with the Giants, coached them for twenty-four years; Jim Lee Howell, an outstanding end with the Giants, coached for seven years; Allie Sherman, a brainy assistant with the Giants, was head coach for eight. They had headline players in every era, including Ken Strong, Mel Hein, Tuffy Leemans, Charley Conerly, Frank Gifford, Y. A. Tittle and many more. The Maras were well-liked by other owners—the official NFL ball used today is called the "Duke" for Wellington Mara—and that never hurt when they wanted to trade. There were no messy labor disputes because players enjoyed the bright lights and commercial potential of the big city. In football, the Giants owned New York.

This was getting to be a bigger and bigger thing and it reached a crescendo in the overtime championship game of 1958, won by the Colts. The game ended dramatically under the lights, electrified the country—and alerted television to football's impact. The football boom was on.

Sam Huff, a very good linebacker playing behind an outstanding line, was deified nationally by the New York-based media (a *Time* cover, a television special) as the hub of the Giants. With an extraordinary series of drafts and trades, and a coaching staff that had Vince Lombardi, Tom Landry and Sherman as assistants, the Giants had broken the stranglehold of the Browns in the Eastern Division. Starting in 1956, they won a championship and five division titles in eight years. The last three were won under Sherman, who replaced Howell in 1961 after the team slipped to third.

Trades for Y. A. Tittle and Del Shofner were instrumental in the rejuvenation under Sherman, but there were signs that the Giant wave was cresting. They were winning with experience and finesse; the flow of talent through the draft had dried up as the opposition's edge in organization began to tell. When the experience and finesse played itself out, which could be any minute, the team could be beached. Recognizing that, the Giants boldly traded tackle Rosey Grier and Huff, who were approaching thirty, for two younger linemen, one of whom had a good season before retiring with an injury while the other was a flop. In 1964 the Giants won two games.

After that disaster the Giants signed Tucker Frederickson, a big fast fullback, the kind of player teams build around and win championships with. He was the first such superstud they had drafted in nine years—the fire commissioner of Philadelphia could have done better than that. The Giants also picked up Earl Morrall in a trade to replace Tittle, and they made a credible comeback to a 7–7 season in 1965. But Frederickson and Morrall both were injured in 1966 and the Giants won one game.

Desperate, they made a deal with the Vikings for quarterback Fran Tarkenton, giving up their top choices in the next two drafts in exchange for instant excitement and respectability. Some critics thought they had mortgaged their future for a very modest present, but Tarkenton was just twenty-six, he could be around for a decade, and quarterbacks like that do not grow in Central Park. The Giants finished 7–7 in his first two seasons, and they were giving every indication of moving on to brighter tomorrows. In the fifth year of rebuilding, 1968, they beat the Cowboys in Dallas and played the Rams to a near standstill in Los Angeles, playing tough with the big boys again. Then they drafted their first superstud lineman in thirteen years, Fred Dryer. He would never play a regular season game for Allie Sherman.

Most teams, when they fall off the top, teams like the Eagles, Redskins, Cardinals, Bears, Lions, Rams, stay down so long that they think they're up when they get respectable. Sherman was bringing the Giants back from nowhere after two losing and three break-even seasons. But Wellington Mara and Giant fans had been up for so long though that they thought respectability was down. With Joe Namath doing his thing in another part of town, it seemed downer. The Giants fired Sherman.

Coaches come and coaches go and, as Mara put it, "Few die on the job." But the ritual sacrifice did serve the useful purpose of showing just how unstuck everyone in the Giants community had become—a parable of collective insanity that has a blood relative in any given NFL city.

The Giants were victims of the same pioneer frugality that did in the Eagles, plus some good old *hubris*. They didn't keep pace with the competition for talent in their own league, depending on their wits to match expanding scouting systems, and when the AFL entered the competition without a license the Giants took the attitude that any college prospect who chose Kansas City over them probably had a bad upbringing and would lay down in the clutch. This was a widespread

conviction in the pre-merger NFL, it never oc-
curring to the established teams that some col-
legians might have the same pioneering spirit
they once had, or that a few of them had attended
classes long enough to figure out that fifty cents
in Kansas City would buy as much fun as ten
cents in New York.

There was every reason for Mara not to take
the AFL too seriously in the early days. From
Yankee Stadium, where the Giants play, he could
look across the Harlem River to the Polo Grounds
—where the Giants used to play and where the
New York Titans were hiding from the public—
and count the house. And Harry Wismer hardly
was a threatening eminence. Wismer's greatest
moment in sports had come years earlier, tele-
casting an NFL game, when he described a runner streaking across the 40, the 45, the 50, the 55-
yard line. Wismer hired Sammy Baugh as his
coach and then wismered around the countryside
boosting the AFL, greeting perfect strangers like
so, "Congratulations, I'm Harry Wismer," and
concocting wild fictions for newspapermen. He
was some piece of work. But the league had to
pay his payroll a few times and he was forced out
of bounds on the 75-yard line.

A syndicate headed by Sonny Werblin bought
the Titans, rechristened them Jets, put them in
Shea Stadium, hired Weeb Ewbank, and com-
menced to move in on the Giants, block by block.
Werblin outbid Mara for fullback Matt Snell

and guard Dave Herman in 1963, and for Joe Namath a year later. Big-time spenders in Buffalo, Houston, Kansas City and San Diego, supported by television money, were signing good ones too. With the financial pressure mounting after the 1965 season, the AFL pinned the commissioner's badge on Al Davis, a successful coach in Oakland and the league's most aggressive recruiter, to fight the NFL to the finish. It was, thanks to Wellington Mara, a quick finish.

Mara bitterly opposed AFL merger proposals, as did the San Francisco 49ers, because they had the territories that the AFL invaded (with Oakland and the Jets). Mara opposed them ideologically as well as geographically, as the old rich vs. the new rich. He actually forbade his players to fraternize with Jets. But such social gamesmanship couldn't stave off the inevitable. The Jets, and Oakland, were recruiting and drawing well.

It came as a shock then when in the spring of 1966 Mara broke an unwritten tampering rule between the warring leagues by signing place kicker Pete Gogolak, who had played out his option in Buffalo. This was an instant replay of the stuffy gentleman reaching across class lines for an irresistible sweet. And that tore it.

Al Davis had been a central character in the cutthroat Keystone Kops chase for college talent, spiriting the youth of America in and out of motels, airports and banks. He had used cunning, brass knuckles and/or money, as the situation warranted. Mara's provocative act even upset his fellow NFL owners, many of whom, bled by the six-figure bonuses, wanted a settlement. But all of their own stars were signed and they couldn't imagine any immediate retaliation by the AFL.

It took Davis three seconds to arrange that. The AFL signed several NFL stars (e.g., John Brodie, Mike Ditka) to huge contracts to go into effect after their current contracts expired. That meant key people on several teams would have divided loyalties. Knowing Davis, the NFL knew he was only starting. In a few days there was peace.

For Mara, it was wonderful. The AFL agreed to pay $25 million to the NFL over a twenty-year period in return for a common draft, realignment, a Super Bowl, inter-league exhibitions and an equal share of TV revenue. The Giants got $10 of the $25 million, the 49ers $8 million. If Mara had his druthers, he'd druther own New York himself—at least he did until he decided in 1971 to abandon the city where he got rich for a proposed new stadium in nearby Hackensack, New Jersey. Still, ten million dollars would buy a lot of other druthers.

It wouldn't buy a defense and that's what Mara needed most. Meanwhile the Jets had their first winning season in 1967 and then went on to win everything in 1968. And Mara began to unravel. He regarded Joe Namath as original sin—sideburns were banned in the Giant dressing room; colorful language still is—and he felt betrayed by newspapers that treated Namath and the Jets seriously. He wrote a letter to the *New York Times* complaining that the Jets were getting preferential treatment. The *Times,* leaving nothing to chance, assigned a man to count the wordage for the season and informed Mara that the Giants still led (2,432,987 to 2,399,106?). Nor did Mara suffer criticism graciously. Elinor Kaine delighted in twitting the Giants in her newsletter, so the Giants vetoed her when she had an opportunity to do her act on the radio station that broadcasts their games. The following summer she sued the Giants (and the Jets and Yale University) when they refused to give her press credentials for the first Giants-Jets exhibition game, at Yale. The suit was settled for one dollar and, with Giant gallantry, a seat in a sexually isolated auxiliary section.

Mara saw the exhibition as an opportunity to put the Jets in their place, prove that their Super Bowl victory over the Colts was a fraud and restore the Giants and the NFL to their rightful place in the Milky Way. All the Giants had to do was win. Namath completed fifteen of seventeen passes and the Jets romped.

A few weeks later, after the Giants lost their fifth exhibition in a row, Mara fired Sherman, who had five years left on a ten-year contract. He hired Alex Webster, an assistant coach who had been an outstanding and popular running back in the '50s and early '60s. The only way to explain this move is in terms of human chemistry, illusion and the supernatural. That's football.

There is no law, of course, that a coach has to stay in office longer than a two-term president. After all only two coaches in the NFL today, Tom Landry of the Cowboys and Hank Stram of the Chiefs, both of whom started with the franchise, have had their jobs longer than eight years. (Witch doctors for soccer teams in Kenya are fired unceremoniously after four straight defeats.) But when there is a changing of the guard by management it should at least hold the promise that the new poor slob is an improvement over the old one. Thus the species may continue its climb from the ooze.

One justified exception to this Darwinian theory of coaching took place in 1970. Dan Reeves, the owner of the Rams, fired George Allen after he had produced five straight winners. Allen, Reeves felt, had virtually stolen the team away from him. He had moved his office and practice setup thirty miles from Los Angeles, had little communication with Reeves and made him feel he was fortunate to be getting free tickets to the games. Reeves, who once fired and then rehired Allen after the players threatened a rebellion, decided that it was his team, that it wasn't fun any more and that he wanted it back. This was reasonable as long as he didn't name Elliot Gould to succeed Allen, just for laughs. Reeves chose Tommy Prothro of UCLA, an inspiration that may provide a championship, but it came too late for fun. Reeves died a few months later.

Wellington Mara wasn't having fun either. The Maras had a splendid tradition, and Wellington Mara, for all the rashes breaking out on him now, had been an enlightened owner in many respects—e.g., he had given tryouts to black quarterbacks years before that became an issue, and he has held the price line to a nine dollar top (compared to thirteen dollars in Denver). But now he couldn't show his face in town without fans snarling at him. The Jets, good grief, were champions. The status of Giant fans, like Mara's, had been devalued. And it would hit the players too. Second is last in the midtown hangouts where their glasses had been filled before with the grapes of laugh.

The fans had been on Sherman for several years, bursting into song to the good-natured if acid strains of "Good-by Allie" late in losing games. It was a message that Sherman himself could appreciate, to a point; a listener, he once took an idea from an equipment manager and the Giants scored a touchdown with it. His children broke him up by singing "Good-by Allie" one night as they went off to bed. But with the passage of seasons the chorus got uglier at Yankee Stadium, until it sounded like a Fred Waring lynch mob. Elinor Kaine brooded that one of those darlings in the stands might really assassinate Sherman.

Losing is all the chemistry that fans need to elect to punt a coach into a vat of sulphuric acid.

In addition Giant fans, spoiled by success, had a feeling of manifest destiny, that the normal cycle of ups and downs shouldn't apply to them. They came to believe that Sherman did nothing but inherit a championship team in 1961 and then, for obscure and perhaps psychotic reasons, jettison their heroes one by one. The Huff trade loomed larger than half a dozen good ones Sherman made (for Tittle, Shofner, Tarkenton, Erich Barnes, Aaron Thomas, Homer Jones, Pete Case and others). Every ten-year-old in the Bronx knew that the Yankees fell from grace because they hadn't competed in the bonus market years before. Every twenty-year-old in Brooklyn knew that the Knickerbockers had spent a lifetime in purgatory because of their front office. But the thirty- and forty-year-old Giant fans made no connection between those barren player drafts and these hard times. "At least," said one, "Webster looks like a coach."

So there was dancing in the streets when Sherman was purged. You would have thought that the Giants sent him to the Rams for Deacon Jones and Merlin Olsen. But no, they did something better. They traded him for an illusion, a potent image of the Great Giant of yesteryear as drawn by Willard Mullin. An all-powerful all-dwarfing all-pro Giant. Alex Webster was the embodiment of that Giant and that time—Big Red, as he was affectionately known, slashing off tackle. Alex Webster, an illusionary time machine, an admitted, somewhat overwhelmed primitive as a coach, was coming off the bench for one of the best coaches in the whole crazy business.

Wellington Mara knew what he was doing. He was guaranteeing himself a comfortable season. It would be more comfortable, and fun, with Webster winning, say, seven games than Sherman winning eight. Who could get mad at Alex Webster? Who could get mad at an owner exercising his constitutional right to have fun?

Two days before the opening game Mara's fun season of 1969 got under way. Webster was given a standing ovation at a pep-rally luncheon and he said, "We're shooting for the Super Bowl, and believe it or not, we're going to be there." Mara said, "The Giants' organization was never more closely unified than it is now. The old magic isn't gone." Magic and illusion. Wake the echoes of the past and march down the field.

The players loved it. In the recorded history of sports, players have been disappointed by a change in coaches three, maybe four times. A new coach is new hope, a chance to show that the old coach didn't know what he was doing when he failed to recognize their extraordinary ability. It means they won't have to listen to the same old spiel, the same threats and pleas—they'll get exciting new ones. Players eagerly welcome a new style in a coach too. When tough Don Shula left the Colts they expressed relief in Don McCafferty's understated approach. When Vince Lombardi succeeded Otto Graham in Washington the Redskins agreed that they needed someone who was tougher on them. For the Giant players, Sherman was cerebral, Webster emotional.

Sherman had run what he called a "total commitment" camp, driving the players hard. But he forgot to totally commit Mara and that was his biggest mistake since the Huff trade. When the Giants lost that last exhibition the players were so irritable that they held a meeting without the coaches, one of those let's-clear-the-air-because-we're-better-than-that-so-buckle-down-Winsocki meetings. Meetings like that can be good or bad, volatile or vaporish, inspiring or depressing. A few hours later Mara made the decision to bring in Webster. One year later Fran Tarkenton stormed out of the dressing room in anger over a move by Webster that resulted in an exhibition defeat, and nothing came of it.

The Giants undeniably were happier with Webster than with Sherman. But the romantic notion that happy players play better than miserable players would soon be dispelled again. The basic fact about professional football players is that they don't care what you do to them if you win. Rub hot coals on their bellies, impugn their masculinity, get down to the nitty-gritty philosophy of Joe Schmidt of the Lions that "Life is a shit sandwich and every day you take another bite." It doesn't matter. Just win.

A fallout of critical hindsight on Sherman billowed through the press. There was, it was said, a generation gap between him and the players, and a motivational gap, and other gaps too humorous to mention. Affectations and neuroses that would be overlooked or deemed colorful in a winner were transformed into fatal shortcomings. Two-four-six-eight, could Sherman motivate? There is one test of whether a coach is motivating his players as individuals: what happens to the players under other coaches. In eight years no players traded or cut by Sherman blossomed elsewhere (although the Colts would make Earl Morrall a star) and many were as useless as a worn-out ball bag. In the year to come under Webster not a single player would be motivated to unsuspected heights. The veteran players who performed were the veteran players who had always performed.

The Giants won their first game under Webster, beating the Vikings with a fourth quarter rally. They carried Webster off the field and trumpeted his earthy virtues. A Giant coach hadn't been carried off the field in such homage since the previous November. Allie Sherman was his name. "He's one of us," said Tucker Frederickson of Webster. "He turned us loose," said tackle Bob Lurtsema.

The inmates were running the asylum and they ran it beautifully—for four weeks. There was an assistant in charge of offense, an assistant in charge of defense, and Webster was in charge of patting fannies. "They're doing 99.9 per cent of the work," the very open and likable Webster said of his staff; he was getting on-the-job training. Then the Giants lost seven games in a row. Lurtsema was benched for three of them.

More important to Mara and other music lovers, no one was singing "Good-by Alex." Instead the appeased fans went after Tarkenton. Get-the-quarterback is another name of the game, and it applies to fans as much as defensive linemen. The Giants won their last three games and that appeased the fans further. The season was a success. The Giants won six games.

Think about that for a moment. The Giants went from seven to six victories and the season was a success. It's like cutting welfare payments and convincing people on welfare that their diets have improved. Wellington Mara got exactly what he figured he would get when he substituted Webster for Sherman: poorer results and fans thinking they got better results. A man who can make six seem more than seven is a man to be reckoned with.

Webster accomplished what he was supposed to accomplish. In September he talked about the Super Bowl. He was cheered. In October he talked about Giant spirit. He was cheered. In November he talked about the lack of talent on the team. He was cheered. In December he talked about next year. He was cheered. He could have recited the rules of parliamentary debate and he would have been cheered.

The players went through the emotional bends with Webster. When they won they won for Alex. When they lost they had let Alex down. And behind his back they whispered that nobody knew what the hell was going on around there.

The NFL came to the Giants' rescue in 1970. The schedule was so soft that you could stick a hand in it right up to the elbow; three teams on it wound up with winning records. And the Browns traded Ron Johnson to the Giants. A superior halfback, Johnson added a dimension of speed that would open up the offense for Fran Tarkenton to maneuver. It was no longer Sherman's team: there were eleven new starters on it since he departed (three ends, three linebackers, three defensive linemen, an offensive tackle, Johnson). They won nine games.

It was an amazing season, a season that made you wonder just how important this coaching is anyway. Fran Tarkenton, like Van Brocklin with the Eagles, took control of the offense after some peculiar things happened.

The Giants lost three of their first four games. After one of the defeats Tarkenton complained that he was getting advice from too many hysterical assistant coaches during the games. In a second defeat the Giants went for a field goal when they had the ball on their opponents' three-inch line; Webster said he didn't realize the ball was that close. The trouble was that nobody on the staff knew more than Tarkenton did. So he took over, improvising game plans and even plays as he went along. He threw five touchdown passes in one game. He brought the team from three touchdowns behind in the fourth quarter to another victory. He did it all, and the Giants won six games in a row. The season was Tarkenton's best, Johnson gained over 1000 yards, Fred Dryer and the top 1970 draft choice, middle linebacker Jim Files, muscled up the defense. And Wellington Mara explained it as though the schedule and Johnson were innocent bystanders. "Alex Webster," he said, "knows how to motivate people."

In 1971 Webster motivated the Giants to a 4—10 season that was such a disaster that not even Mara could make it seem like anything else. Tarkenton, Dryer and safety man Spider Lockhart, the team leaders, bickered with Webster and Mara in the press. Mara rehired Webster, saying that he was, gulp, still learning. Tarkenton and Dryer demanded to be traded and were. The Giants were rebuilding, again, by getting rid of their best players. They replaced the Eagles as the laughingstock of the league.

Which is the end of this tale of two cities, moral being that it could be a tale of every NFL city. In Oakland, Al Davis plots mad schemes while his team is divided over its two quarterbacks, Daryle Lamonica and George Blanda. In St. Louis the brothers Bidwell who run the Cardinals couldn't agree on firing Charley Winner when he was a loser in 1969 but they could agree on firing him when he won in 1970. George Allen went to Washington and immediately traded the Jefferson Memorial, the Department of Commerce and thirty-four draft picks for a handful of aging Rams, who got them into the playoffs. The Saints were going through a shakeup that suggested they were studying the history of the Eagles. In Houston Bud Adams fired his coach, Chuck Hughes, because he wouldn't get rid of his equipment manager.

City by city the evidence mounts that touchdowns rather than fumbles are accidents. Joe Schmidt is a profound fellow.

Play diagrams are essential to any self-respecting book about football. They add a ring of authority, and they look good—Xs, Os, dotted lines, wavy lines, arrows breaking into the clear. For all we know, this portfolio of originals may be all-pro. Television is big on diagrams too. But most people notice that that crushing block that the O puts on the X in the diagram usually winds up looking like a lunge and an elbow on film, and that the arrow represents a runner whose instinctive wiggle and tackle-breaking strength somehow do not come across on paper or blackboards. One coach once spent a half hour diagramming complex new defenses for his team, put down his chalk and said, "And if you understand that you're smarter than I am." This may be worth remembering the next time they try to dazzle you with Xs and Os.

"The Star-Spangled Banner Formation" is mandatory in the NFL. The O team here has a man offsides. The penalty is the same whether he is nervous, absent-minded or making a political protest: 15 yards and compulsory attendance at the half-time show.

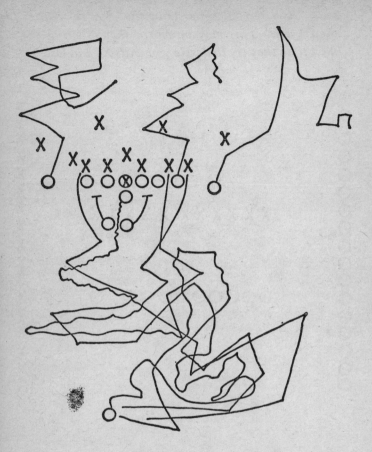

Here's a play made famous by Fran Tarkenton,
Craig Morton, Norm Snead and other quarterbacks. It's called "The Scramble Out of Field
Goal Range Play." It's used on third down anywhere from the opponents' 20- to 30-yard line and
it winds up at their 45 or 50.

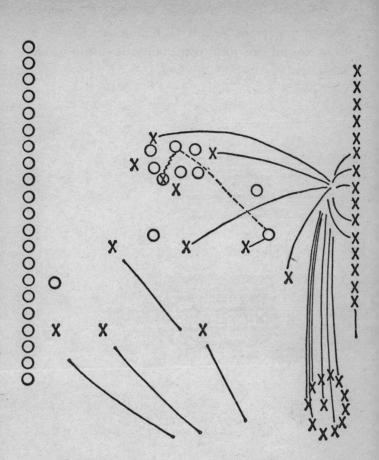

This is the well-known "Carry the Coach Off the Field Special." Although his admirers insist that Vince Lombardi conceived it for championship games, Walter Camp first used it at Yale. Notice how the substitutes rush to beat the regulars to the coach.

For all you great X and O gamesmen, here is a page to fill in your own fantastic unstoppable fantasies.

9. CLEAR
BUT LOUD

The Colonists insisted on using flankers and men in motion. The British, who were unbeaten with their simple power plays, said that was against the rules. The Boston T Party followed and the nation was plunged into the Revolution Bowl.

"Give me football or give me death," said Patrick Henry, the All-American from Virginia.

"I have but one life to give for my team," said the great Nathan Hale.

"Don't pass 'til you see the whites of their eyes," ordered a quarterback in the playoffs at Lexington.

Meanwhile, in France, promoter Benjamin Franklin, trying to raise money for the new franchise, whispered to an important lady, "Dancing is a contact sport. Football is a collision sport."

And at Valley Forge coach George Washington said at half time, "Winning isn't everything. It's the only thing."

Thus professional football was born. A grateful people called a Continental Congress to form a country the game could be proud of.

THE medium, said Marshall McLuhan, is the message. And sometimes the message that filters through the medium of television is too clear. One night in the summer of 1970 there was such a time.

The Giants were playing the Steelers an exhibition game in Pittsburgh. An exhibition game is a scrimmage that the NFL calls a pre-season game so it can charge fans regular-season prices. Fran Tarkenton, like many veterans who sit out whole or parts of these charades, was not going to play, so the American Broadcasting Company had a brilliant idea. They lassoed a microphone around his neck on the sideline.

Tarkenton, his legs crossed casually, was glib and chatty in conversations with Howard Cosell, the mouth that roars, and Don Meredith, the former Dallas Cowboy. He commented about this, that and the other quarterback, adhering to the jock code that the most heinous thing you can say about another jock is that he's a fine player.

So there were jockular exchanges about the difficulties the Giants were having on the field, which were considerable. Dick Shiner, Tarkenton's backup, was having a particularly rough go and Tarkenton said that, well, he was throwing into a wind most of the time. Meredith chuckled, Tarkenton grinned and they were having just one big old laugh between quarterbacks.

And the next day Pete Rozelle said that would be the end of that.

With good reason, from Pete Rozelle's view. The Tarkenton number might have been great show biz but it also might have undermined the product that the NFL and ABC were selling. The product was exhibition football at nonexhibition prices. The message that filtered through the verbiage was the truth of that. No matter how often it might be suggested in newspapers that exhibitions were not of grave national concern, the football fan, with his television blinkers on, had to see it before he could believe it. Seeing Tarkenton sitting on the sideline with his legs crossed casually was irrefutable evidence that the game wasn't life or death, that it was like those exhibition baseball games when you couldn't care less if your team lost to the Kansas City B squad. The game could still be enjoyed but would you want to pay regular prices for it? Some day you might not.

Which illustrates the essential thing about television and football. The picture is the message.

No amount of NFL fog, of which there is an endless supply, can obscure the game. This is a tribute to the indomitable spirit of the football fan too. He's taken everything the NFL can send at him and still he comes back.

Pro football as we know it is television's baby. Television created the AFL, underwriting it until it could stand on its own feet. Television created the interest that fills most stadiums most of the time. Television also has created a new breed of fan, the fan who may never see a live game because of the advance sellouts. Of the 60 to 70 million fans who watch the Super Bowl on television, perhaps a million and a half attend games in person during the season.

The Sunday shut-ins miss out on the madding crowd, the panorama of the stadium, the bracing spectacle and the bad hot dogs, but they see the game in a dimension not possible from the 50-yard line. They see the instant replays, slow-motion reruns, split screens and other electronic razzle-dazzle that isolate the bad and the beautiful from the clamor of bodies. A sense of the whim and/or responsibility in a play can be established on TV, there are friezes of animal fury and grace, and the 12–15 minutes of actual action in a game are fleshed out to a nearly continuous montage.

But there are dues to be paid by the shut-ins. They have to listen to the NFL's cheerleading corps, the television announcers.

Ideally an announcing team should have a play-by-play man who can supplement the picture with a clear narrative in unhysterical English, and a color man who can interpret what is happening in plain English. Both of them would add levity when possible, inject notes and sketches on personalities when appropriate, and keep an eye out for the mad doings of people on and off the field. They wouldn't belabor you with statistics and they would know when to shut up and let the action tell the story. Perhaps we will live to hear it.

That kind of performance would in the long run be the best possible promotion for pro football. But the NFL and television and sponsors demand the hype of jock interpreters, who infect the play-by-play pros with their gobbledygook. What you usually get from a jock announcer is a combination of the television and football mentalities, which is like crossing a used car salesman with a professor of Sanskrit. He talks a lot and you don't know what he's talking about. He interprets Sanskrit in Sanskrit. The television mentality shills for his product, football, by apologizing for it and ingratiating himself with the viewer at every opportunity. The jock mentality retreats behind jargon, cliché and myth, and doesn't have the training or inclination to conduct a coherent interview.

Jack Craig, TV columnist for the *Boston Globe*

and the *Sporting News,* cited three of many examples of such game coverage last season:

1. Pat Summerall in the 49ers-Cowboys game excused Mel Phillips' drop of a potential key interception by citing the "remarkable" fact that he was even playing, due to a bad hand. The remarkable aspect of the play was Dallas' good luck that Phillips dropped the ball.

2. Al DeRogatis cited Johnny Unitas' "courage" on a third down pass over the middle that was broken for a long touchdown against the Bengals after the quarterback had misfired on two previous passes.

3. Frank Gifford referred to Craig Morton as "one of the offensive heroes of the game" as he introduced the quarterback in a post-game show after the Cowboys-Detroit game.

The viewer knows that a football can be dropped for no particular reason, that Unitas does not have to reach for inner valor when passing and that Morton had just played an embarrassingly bad game against Detroit.

Other jocks on television see so many "remarkable" and "courageous" things happening on any given Sunday that the English language is debased to a duffle bag of clichés and adjectives: "great" 2-yard runs are followed by "booming" 38-yard punts. Worse, the jocks have wrought havoc in the land by spreading the mystique of strategy, game plans, Mo Mentum and goodness knows what else. In recent years they haven't babbled as much as they used to about "zig-outs" and "banana patterns" and whatnot because the instant replays showed that these mysterious pass routes generally consisted of a head fake or a guy running to an open spot, throwing up his hands and yelling for the ball.

DeRogatis, once a fine tackle with the Giants, is, alas, the biggest disaster that ever hit pro football. As a radio broadcaster for the Giants for many years he popularized the concept of the color man as colorless pedant. He spouted jargon and algebraic defensive alignments at a machine-gun clip. This convinced his audience that he knew what was going on, presumably reassuring them that everything was under control. De-Rogatis felt a compulsion to predict plays too. Occasionally he was right—he does know football —and if the Giants didn't follow his orders there was consternation among fans: what was wrong with the Giants anyway? If they ran the play he predicted six plays later, DeRogatis would be assured by the play-by-play man that he had done it again. A whole generation of Giant fans, their minds addled beyond repair, have been trying to emulate him. Now a TV network man, DeRogatis persists in the same tradition with less success. This is how he sounds:

"The Bills were in an overshifted odd defense with the strong-side linebacker blitzing and the weakside safety in a rotating zone, and Csonka was stopped for no gain."

An end run failed.

"Johnson tried to hit Levias in the seam but the middle linebacker hit the back coming out of the backfield trying to flood the right zone, leaving the safety free to roam."

He dropped the ball.

"On the previous play, you'll remember, they double-teamed the flanker, so this time Unitas went to his upback on a flareout but the Patriots were in a prevent defense with looping tackles."

He didn't see the open man.

"Hadl automaticked and they went on set but the short trap fake on the weak side didn't fool Davidson."

Somebody forgot to block the defensive end.

"That time the tight end crossed with the split end and the flanker ran an up, leaving the flat open for a zig-out on a delayed count, and Griese hit them underneath again."

A 6-yard completion.

"It looked like the tackle and end were gaming from the stack defense and when Little cut back he was met unexpectedly by the linebacker who read the key."

He fumbled.

DeRogatis is by no means the only offender in this area but he perfected the form. Coaches walk out on that stuff in football clinics. Even they want to smile once in awhile.

Curt Gowdy and the late Paul Christman were the top television team in the '60s because Christman could translate football jargon into English, because he didn't try to overpower the game with his expertise and because he didn't treat it like an Easter sunrise service. He would occasionally explain a quarterback's alternatives, and when the quarterback elected to pick a third to fourth alternative Christman would mock his own standing as resident genius. Christman probably had as much to do with the survival of the AFL in the early years as anyone because even NFL die-hards, who were the overwhelming majority, recognized that he was giving them something they couldn't get anywhere else—a good-humored, relaxed yet informative reading of a game of football.

Gowdy of NBC is a professional with an eye for the offbeat detail. He had the security and instinct to defer to Christman, like a good straight man. He has to strain with the bland Kyle Rote. Ray Scott of CBS does an excellent job with a precise economical style that builds slowly in tensile strength as a game rolls toward an exciting climax, with the action and crowd noise building naturally and dramatically.

Don Meredith had a big rookie year for ABC on its Monday night extravaganza in 1970, also because he wasn't awed by the game. Countrified, open and enthusiastic, Meredith came across as a Dizzy Dean with a touch of grammar. He made such a strong impression that ABC reportedly kept him from returning to the Cowboys in 1971, a break for ABC and the Cowboys. Anyone who can get as excited over Fair Hooker's name as another touchdown, as Meredith did, has a sense of proportion you don't hardly get any more.

ABC's overall sense of proportion wasn't quite as winsome. Trying to do too much, they shot so many replays and so many announcers at you that there were times when they sounded like they were trying to jam their own telecast. The game could barely get through. Meredith was accompanied by a play-by-play man, Keith Jackson, and the unsinkable Howard Cosell. What they needed most was Dick Cavett to moderate the show. What they got was Frank Gifford as a replacement for Jackson.

Cosell is an electronic phenomenon unto himself. Television sportscasting was at such a low ebb that he rose to the top just by standing up.

Owing to sponsor pressures, local chauvinism and the attitude that fun and games weren't important enough to cover intelligently, sportscasters generally have been either cheerleaders or eunuchs. Or, recently, jocks. Cosell barged in and, with a flair for the tabloid sensationalism of the '20s, established himself as a giant among pygmies. He isn't, as Muhammad Ali often told him, as dumb as he looks, because he also exploited a second weakness of television, its tendency to make bigger stars of the reporters who cover stars than the stars themselves. Cosell is the star of his own interviews, most of which are conducted like the Nuremberg trials.

These distortions and a gift for humorless nonstop overstatement of the obvious have turned Cosell into a parody of himself. To his credit he has taken unpopular stands and been more imaginative and aggressive than his competition, rare TV lapses into something approaching journalism. But when he does an event he reverts to the parody and overpowers the event. He is not there to supplement the event, it is there to supplement him.

This apparently is good show biz. So is the screeching of monkeys in a zoo, although the monkeys have the sense to screech monosyllabic screeches. Cosell's baroque delivery, full of "perusals" and "ferrets" and the like, inspired this "Open Letter to Howard Cosell" by one Harry Felsenstein of Brooklyn:

In promulgating your esoteric cogitations, or articulating your superficial sentimentalities and amicable, philosophical or psychological observations, beware of platitudinous ponderosity.

Let your conversational comprehensibleness be a coalescent consistency and a concatenated cogency. Eschew all conglomerations of flatulent garrulity, jejune babblement and asinine affectations.

Let your extemporaneous descantings and unpremeditated expatiations have intelligibility and veracious vivacity, without rodomontade or thrasonical bombast.

Sedulously avoid all polysyllabic profundity, pompous prolixity, psittaceous vacuity, ventriloquial verbosity, and ventrose vapidity. Shun double-entendres, prurient jocosity, and pestiferous profanity, obscurant or apparent.

As positive as the reaction to Meredith was, it was negative to Cosell because of his stridency. He doesn't clarify or amplify, he CLARIFIES and AMPLIFIES. What comes at you is: THIS IS ME, HOWARD COSELL, WHO JUST THIS AFTERNOON HAD LUNCH WITH CHOU EN-LAI, TELLING YOU THAT THAT PASS WAS OVERTHROWN! ! ! yes, we know, howard, we just saw it.

So anxious was Cosell to TELL US WHAT'S GOING ON that he often misled us. When Leroy Kelly of the Browns was contained by the Jets, Cosell told us that he was no factor in the game. A player of Kelly's stature is always a factor, even if it isn't obvious. Cosell deals in the obvious, as he did when he made excuses for a bad night Johnny Unitas had—later, off the air, overstating that "Unitas is washed up and he knows it." He made excuses for Bart Starr too, and in Green Bay he ingratiated himself with the audience that was up in arms about him by giving a cloying this-is-the-very-ground-on-which-He-stood eulogy to Vince Lombardi. And although he has been critical of television shills, when the Chiefs were routing the Colts in the first half of a game, ending it then and there, Cosell shilled by being strangely mute. One had the sensation of a jackhammer that had sat down to dinner suddenly leaving the house.

The highlight of the ABC season was yet to come. Cosell disappeared altogether in the second half of a game between the Giants and the Eagles in Philadelphia. On a cold and windy night he took a few drinks and got sick to his stomach, all over the booth, some over Don Meredith's pants leg. Many football fans, unable to stomach Cosell's combination of gall and treacle, knew just how he felt.

The instant replays and slow-motion reruns on television may be contributing to the breakdown of law and order in the country. Scarcely a week goes by when officials aren't caught making mistakes that can't be appealed to a higher court. The Giants lost a game in New Orleans last sea-

son when a touchdown catch that was clearly in bounds was disallowed. The fine line between pass interference and a good aggressive play gives officials the most trouble. A pass play seems to make them think they are competing in a flag-throwing contest. Offensive holding on pass protection is another fine-line area. Winston Hill of the Jets found that he had fewer penalties called on him when he stopped wearing gloves that stood out in the crowd. Nevertheless the officials do a good job overall and a better understanding of their signals, as shown in the following illustrations, should add to the enjoyment of spectators.

So I missed one. Crucify me.

For $50 I could miss another one.

Don't ask me. I got this off a temple Good grief, the
I just work here. at Angkor Wat. Eagles-Steelers again.

Simon says do this, Peace—make love, Take a left at the 20,
do that, do . . . not war. then a right.

10. FUGUE FOR
GRID HORNS

God: Noah!

Noah: Yes, Lord.

God: I want you to build a raft.

Noah: A raft?

God: A raft. Make it a hundred and twenty yards long and fifty-three yards wide, and, oh, a couple of feet thick. Throw some dirt on top of it and plant some grass seed.

Noah: That's a big raft, Lord.

God: It's a floating football field, Noah. The flood is coming. We can't call the games on account of flood, can we?

Noah: Yes, Lord. I mean, no, Lord.

God: Take them two-by-two, Noah. You can start with the Lions and the Rams.

Noah: Uh-huh.

God: Then the Dolphins and the Colts.

Noah: The Broncos and the Bears, the Falcons and the Eagles.

God: That's right. Good, Noah.

Noah: The Bengals and the Cardinals. . . . Lord?

God: Yes?

Noah: I like the Falcons with the points.

God: You're on, Noah.

It is time to clear up the baffling mystery of who is the betting commissioner of the country. He is Pete Rozelle.

Officially Rozelle is the commissioner of pro football. Every three or four years he opens the envelopes with the sealed bids from the networks for television rights. Annually he reads the name of the first college player picked in the draft. He checks out new territories for expansion and draws up schedules. And he makes appearances at dinners for Bart Starr. Can that be it?

Don't be silly. His real job is to maintain the integrity of professional football. The integrity of the game is vital because the big question today is: "What's the point spread?" If the game is honest, the fans will keep betting. And if they keep betting, the NFL will prosper from here to eternity.

An enormous amount of money is bet on pro football. Weekly estimates range from the gross national product of Tanzania to the deficit in the

U.S. budget. Nobody knows how much. But one of the many misconceptions about gambling is that if the figure is, say, $10 billion, that means that football fans are being duped into financing illicit underworld operations, the corruption of public officials and so on for the whole $10 billion. The fact is that if the figure is $10 billion, an outside figure, the service charge is about $500 million, which is barely enough to keep the bookies in pinky rings. (They would have to handle some $200 billion to clear $10 billion. A bettor usually lays 11-10 odds with a bookie. This means that if he wins he wins ten dollars and if he loses he loses eleven dollars. If the bettor wins one bet and loses another, the bookie wins one dollar, or 5 per cent of the $20 bet. It adds up.)

All this activity, and the interest in football and the trust in bookies that it implies, has a tremendous influence on the game. Without it the NFL might be in serious trouble.

Bombarded with games on television, just seven of his own team's per season, the football fan has become sophisticated to the point where he can distinguish between a good game and a bad game. The novelty then of simply having a game to look at isn't enough to command his attention for fourteen full regular season games. There are just so many times you can take the Broncos and the Falcons and the Bears for three solid hours if you don't live in Denver, Atlanta and Chicago, and maybe if you do too. If the fan didn't turn on the set every time there's a game, or if he turned it off in the third quarter of every bad game, NFL TV ratings would plummet. A dialogue on whether the game has peaked would begin. Advertisers, paying $70,000 a minute, would desert the sinking ship for the roller derby. The financial structure of professional football, built on the foundation of television revenue, would crumble. Players, forced to take salaries cut in half, would quit. Pro football would be obsolete before Dave Meggyesy's revolution got to it.

We have been saved from this fate worse than death by gambling. Bookies report that there is three times as much action on televised games as on non-televised games.

Football is a beautiful game to bet on. It's easy to make yourself think you can evaluate one team against another and it's easy to weigh that against the point spread. For a few dollars you can have something going for you: a gut-rooting interest. A football game you are betting on is like a three-hour horse race punctuated by favorable and unfavorable caprices of man and nature. You are alive on every play, you agonize or exult during every TV rerun, lending an alternating current of gloom and glory to even the routine happenings. Winning, you hang in smugly to the sweet end to savor your expertise. Losing, you hang in with joyful self-abuse while clucking epithets at the figurines on the screen. You are a self-made captive audience and you are the NFL's best friend.

At a game itself the bettor generates a similar dimension of involvement, win or lose, close game or rout. Throughout the afternoon his head jerks back and forth from the field to the scoreboard (read: tote board). Murmurs and roars punctuate every new score, even when they are in such dreary outposts as New Orleans or Boston. And when the home team is losing convincingly, on the scoreboard, and the stadium is a tomb, who but the man with points can sustain hope, electricity and excitement? Even the handful of non-bettors may settle for the moral victory of winning the game-within-a-game of the point spread. In the last few seasons such hopeless causes as the Patriots and Falcons have redeemed their fans and nation-wide supporters by leading the standings in winning games with the points. A name of the game not to be overlooked.

In appreciation for your business the book-maker provides useful services that Pete Rozelle couldn't arrange without him. Accurate injury reports, for one. If Gale Sayers sneezes in Chicago they say *gesundheit* in Las Vegas and thirty seconds later you can't bet on the Bears game in Miami. The NFL gave up trying to get accurate reports on injuries because too many coaches lied about them, some by not listing them at all, and some by camouflaging casualties under such vague headings as "questionable" and "very questionable" and "doubtful" and "probable." Coaches like to play this game-within-a-game because they feel they might get an edge on a team that has prepared on a false assumption of his strength. Al Davis doesn't let out-of-town reporters talk to players in the Oakland dressing room during the week for this reason, while other coaches and general managers of his persuasion go through less transparent dances. But if the Lions show up without cornerback Lem Barney and the opposition doesn't capitalize on that, or if, through the routine miracle of overnight healing, a supposedly injured Gene Washington materializes in the 49ers lineup and the opposition doesn't adjust to that, the opposition is in so much trouble that it doesn't make any difference if those stars play or not. For the bettor there is one danger on injury reports, even accurate ones: that he will make too much of them. Many a bet has been made and blown on the basis of injuries. Usually it takes an injury to a very key player—a Namath, a Butkus, a Bell, a Sayers—to influence the outcome of a game, and the odds are adjusted when players of that caliber are out. But frequently a result isn't influenced materially even when a star is out. Anyone who thinks he can divine these things better than the bookies—who can be as mystified and mystifying as the coaches and players—should be put on a short leash.

The bookie furnishes one final service that the NFL doesn't. It is called the two-minute rule. If a game is halted with two minutes or more left to play, regardless of the score, all bets are off. The practical value of the rule may be insignificant but as a last-straw-of-hope it is unbeatable. It is not beyond a bettor, having lost bets on excruciating freak plays, to root for a riot or a natural disaster to rescue himself.

As the commissioner, Pete Rozelle has admirably fulfilled his obligation to keep the faithful faithful and the bettors betting.

In 1962 he suspended Paul Hornung and Alex Karras for a year, Hornung for betting on his team, the Packers, and for providing information to gamblers; Karras for associating with unsavory characters in his bar. The danger in a player's betting on himself is that, like any bettor, he will lose and get himself in such a bind that he might be tempted to bet against himself. The danger in a player's providing tips to gamblers is that, players being notoriously poor selectors, the gamblers would have no chance of winning, which might tempt them to try to arrange a fix next time. In the main gamblers like to think they get an edge to exploit when a bit of information that usually can be found at the bottom of news stories—Charlie Gorilla has an ingrown toenail—is casually volunteered by a player. Gamblers, like presidents and preachers, are jock sniffers.

In 1969 Rozelle put on a symbolic show of force that reinforced his power as betting commissioner. He demonstrated just how straight the game is by ordering Joe Namath to sell his interest in a bar, acting on the information that the district attorney's office was going to close down the joint (which proved wrong) because underworld figures were hanging out there (which was right). But bets were being placed from telephones in the bar and bookies were shaken by the potential for a scandal that would ruin business.

They did criticize Rozelle's handling of one case though. A story broke during the week before the 1970 Super Bowl that Len Dawson, quarterback of the Chiefs, was involved with a big-time gambler in Detroit, where he hadn't been as a player in eleven years. The Super Bowl is like Christmas shopping at Macy's for bookies, the biggest one-shot of the year, and for a few nervous hours it was touch and go whether the game would be taken down as a betting proposition. Dawson denied any wrongdoing although he admitted that this gambler, whom he said he knew as a businessman, would call him from time to time to check out reports on his ailing knee and on his mental well-being after the death of his father. Dawson said he attached no importance to the calls except the concern of an old acquaintance.

What stunned the bookies was the revelation that despite previous investigations of Dawson, Rozelle's investigators had no knowledge of his relationship with Mr. Detroit. This did not say much for the NFL's sleuthing.

Dawson had taken lie-detector tests several years before after bookies had alerted Rozelle to what they thought were strange doings in Kansas City. The Chiefs were taken off the betting line for several games because a few heavy bettors were right too often. Dawson cleared himself. Like many strong defense-oriented teams, the Chiefs would rout some opponents and have fits trying to score on others. It's possible that somebody figured out whom the others would be.

One owner in the '50s was fined upwards of $5000 by the league for betting on his team in a big game, which he won. Years later word raced through the bookie network that he bet $200,000 on a game, and lost. If an owner can't get better inside information than that, who can?

Since people want to bet, and since no one has been able to stop them, the city of New York, first in the country to legalize off-track betting on horse racing, eventually will try to expand to football and other games. Rozelle, naturally, opposes it, fearing that legal betting, unlike all the illegal betting going on, would deflower innocent fans and players alike. The bookies may make him their Man of the Year for that.

Is there hanky-panky going on in pro football? Isolated incidents in the last twenty years that were unprovable reportedly are on file with the NFL. It is naïve to believe that a point-shaving fix couldn't, or doesn't, happen once in awhile now. It would almost be disappointing if fantasies of larceny didn't occur to some stout hearts occasionally. But the bookies trust the game, and bank it, and that's a powerful endorsement. Games are fixed by gamblers for profit and profit can only be made by betting and bookies are sensitive to the suspicious fluctuations in odds that heavy betting induces because they are the victims. If it happens often enough, they won't take bets on the team in question, and that doesn't happen often. Nevertheless imaginary rumors of conspiracies abound—invariably spread by losing bettors—and some cynics bet with the firm conviction that they are trying to pick the team choreographed to win. It's as good as any other system to dope out a game.

Where there is so much ego, emotion, money and ignorance at play, there are bound to be thousands of misconceptions to feed the frustration and confusion of losers. Perhaps the most popular of them is the one that slanders bookies as mere gamblers. They do gamble—soda jerks drink sodas, don't they?—but in their roles as bankers the incidence of knavery is certainly less than it is on Wall Street.

About one game per weekend falls on or near the point spread and yet even that is the source of two misconceptions. One is that an all-knowing presence out there in the Nevada desert has the game worked out on an abacus. Not so. The oddsmakers overestimate and underestimate their point spreads by more than a touchdown far more often than they get within a touchdown of the result. Occasionally they pick a spread that is incomprehensible, but their image of omniscience intimidates bettors from challenging them. Their job isn't to calculate a game to the point anyway —it is to calculate a spread that will stimulate betting on both sides so that the bookies will clear their 5 per cent of the gross at least. It's a volume business. Sometimes the betting tendencies of the public are weighed in with the relative merits of the team in a given calculation; if the public is consistently sending in money on the Packers, for example, the oddsmakers will adjust the odds to stimulate betting against them.

The second misconception about games that land exactly on the point spread—a three-point favorite winning by three points—is that the bookie rakes in everything like a blackjack dealer with an ace and a king. To the contrary, the danger is then greatest for him to lose his pinky ring. If a game opens at three points, and the odds get driven up to three and a half or four points, and then get driven down to two and a half or two, as money is bet on both sides, the bookie can get trapped in the middle if the favorite does win by three. He has to pay the bettors who took three and a half or four and he has to pay the bettors who gave two and a half or two, and he breaks even with the bettors who gave three. It doesn't happen often but it happens. If the oddsmakers hit too many on the nose they could put everyone out of business.

The best-known oddsmaker in the country is Jimmy (The Greek) Snyder of Las Vegas. What Snyder really is is a promotions man, and his greatest promotion is himself. Like a magician with a clever line of abracadabra patter, Snyder injected show biz into his pronouncements on Super Bowl point spreads and, *voilà*, he gained fame as an all-knowing presence in the desert. After picking the Packers to beat the Raiders by fifteen points in the second Super Bowl, Snyder broke down the spread point by abracadabra point: Bart Starr was worth two points over Daryle Lamonica, the Packer receivers were worth two points, their defense eight points (four in the secondary), their specialty teams one point, their experience one and a half points, Vince Lombardi one and a half points. The Raiders got a point for their kicking game. Add it and subtract it and it comes to fifteen. "Their team speed," Snyder said authoritatively, "is even." Had he clocked both teams from poolside in Vegas? Why quibble? Fifteen points was the spread and if Jimmy Snyder could analyze it down to the last cleat, you had to give him points for that.

What else have the oddsmakers done lately? With the points, they have been off by two touchdowns or more in four of the six Super Bowls. This may be better than the charlady-hatpin system of winner picking, but not much.

There are two basic ways to bet pro football: on individual games or on groups of games on parlay cards. Theoretically a bettor who bets one game a week has the best chance to win, because one game is easier to pick than two. The trouble with this method is that if you win a few bets in a row you begin to believe, fatally, that you have the thing licked. You start betting on two or more games for higher stakes and in no time at all you're hocking the family heirlooms.

Theoretically you can't win by betting on parlay cards. The odds are terrible. You get 10—1 to pick four out of four winners when the actual odds are 16—1. On the other hand, when you lose you've missed out only on 10—1 instead of 16—1. There are two advantages to betting on parlay cards: more games therefore more action, less money bet—because the odds are so stacked against winning—therefore less money lost.

There are dozens of betting rules for the avid gamesman, all invaluable in making you forget that you don't have the slightest notion of what's going on. Here are a few of them:

Never bet against the home team when it is the underdog by two or more touchdowns. The logic behind this is that the home team will respond to the urging of wives, friends and other critics to make the game at least respectable. Notice, however, that this is not advice to bet *on* the home team when it is the underdog by two or more touchdowns, because usually nothing but the funny ball can help a home team that's that bad.

Ignore the results of the previous week's games.
The logic behind this is that too many bettors
are influenced by the most recent scores, especially when they have seen the latest game on television. Many bettors misread the point spread because they operate under the false assumption
that if the Broncos were sensational beating the
Redskins this week, and the Redskins ripped the
Saints last week, then the Broncos should waste
the Saints next week. It doesn't work that way. For
the majority of teams that are not crushingly
strong or pitifully weak, the results of games between them usually are determined by the special
matchups of that game, as well as the crazy players and the funny ball. Are one team's ends too
much for the other team's secondary? Can one
team's quarterback handle the other team's rush?
Does the seventh moon of Saturn cross with one
coach's game plan? Is one punter's wife threatening to divorce him unless he gets home from prac-
tices before midnight?

*Don't bet on an underdog unless you think it
will win the game.* If a team is an underdog by
ten points, don't bet on it because you think it will
lose by three or seven. Bet on it only if you think
it is good enough to beat the favorite. To win the
whole game, as they say. The logic behind this is
that it helps you eliminate games to bet on. Betting on too many games is like betting on flies

landing on a lump of sugar. But, of course, you might do better with the flies, unless the fix is in.

Bet against the smart money. The smart money is the money that challenges the spread, that bets so much on a particular game that the odds go from, say, four to six points. The logic to this system is that, over the course of the season, the oddsmaker will be right more often than the smart money. You're betting with him.

Computers have invaded the visceral domain of betting too. But when someone claims he has a game figured to a third decimal point, run, don't walk. The following familiar litany comes from an outfit that staged an NFL computerized game on radio last year: "The think machine had nothing to be ashamed of, except the final score."

The machine had no character.

STOP ACTION

An Intimate Football Diary
by a Nobody

April 1

An NFL contract smells like lime and clean
sweat socks. I got mine in the mail today. I used
to tear the envelope open to see the magic number. One year, my fourth, I think, I was so anxious
that I tore the top of the contract right off. I was
sick for three days. The number was $18,500, the
same as the year before, and I was going to sign.
But when I tore the contract I figured they'd
know how eager I was, and I thought the best
thing was to sit tight until they sent me another
one. Ten days later I got another contract, for
$20,000. The bastards. It was the first time I
hadn't signed the first contract they sent me. For
the next four years I threw the first contract
away automatically and I always got a $1500
raise. If I had any nerve I would've torn up a few
of those second contracts, but if I had that much
nerve I wouldn't have been a professional backup
quarterback.

So I signed my contract today for $24,000, down from last year's $26,000. A backup quarterback has to be careful. If you make too much money they'll dump you.

June 6

I got a call from Johnnycake Lane today. I've been expecting it. Almost waiting for it.

"How much you getting?" Johnnycake asked.

He's very subtle.

I told him I was getting $22,000.

"They cut you again?"

"Yeah," I said. "Hell, I only played nine minutes last year."

"When can I expect the dough?"

"At camp," I said.

"Send me a hundred now, okay? You'll give me the other nine hundred later."

We have a deal, Johnnycake and me. He gets 5 per cent of my salary. He's not too good at arithmetic—I've beaten him out of a few hundred bucks a year for the last three years, since we made the deal—but he's a helluva place kicker. I'll give him $50 a week until the last player cut, then $500 if I make the squad.

They drafted a quarterback on the second round this year. The deal is my insurance.

July 15

You're never ready for the opening day of training. I used to run all winter and spring on the beach to get ready. It never helped. Shocker was spending his winter and spring figuring out how to torture us. Joe Shocky—we call him Shocker—is our coach. I guess Shocker is the toughest coach in the business. His motto is "The name of the game is pain." Shocker uses an electric cattle prod on the linemen and a cat-o'-nine-tails on the backs and ends. But he's a sentimental old guy. Breaks down and cries every time he draws blood. We hate him now but five months from now we'll love him.

July 19

We lost our first rookie today. Stanley Stanley was his name. Good kid, a defensive tackle from Desire U. Shocker liked him. "Notice how you don't get a peep out of him," Shocker said one day. "I like those kind. Not many of them around any more." The kid walked out after the morning practice. He left a note saying he couldn't stand the smell of the factory in town. They've been making blueberry pies for a week and the kid couldn't take it any more. Shocker was philosophical. "If he couldn't take the blueberry," Shocker said, "he damn sure wouldn't get through the cinnamon next week. And the pumpkin. We'll separate the men from the boys by the time we get through the pumpkin."

We had our first grass drill today. About eight of us. Doc Greenie, the trainer, doesn't pass out any pills until the first exhibition game. Shocker's orders. Some of us vets have a little grass patch down in the corner of the field. A very *special* grass patch. You haven't lived until you do fifty side-straddle hops on that NFL Gold. Damnedest thing though is that crazy end, Max Miracle. Max gets high on salt tablets. Every time Shocker growls, "Don't forget your salt tablets," Max grins like a maniac.

July 27

I gave Johnnycake his third $50 today. He's starting to come through, and just in time. The rookie quarterback can throw the air out of the damn ball. Name's Steve Six. They gave him the number 6 and everyone calls him Six-Six. I'm counting on the coaching staff to fill the kid's head with so much crap that they confuse him for three years. There's less to this game than meets the eye.

Anyway I got my annual pre-exhibition season interview in the *Globe*. All about how I still want to be first-string in my eleventh year, still think I got a shot. "I wouldn't be playing otherwise." But if I couldn't beat out our No. 1, Jim Dandy, I'd be satisfied to help the team as the No. 2. Jeezus. If

Dandy got hurt I'd kill myself. When he gets a cold I worry. I feel like feeding him hot chicken soup. I get sick when he gets hit.

Johnnycake gave me a good plug in the story. Said I was indispensable to him as a holder, the best holder in the business. That's why I pay for insurance. Understand? Johnnycake can't kick with anyone else holding. I may do a book on holding. They've done them on everything else.

July 30

Eight rookies got cut today. I guess the pumpkin pie got them.

August 2

We started a three-day holiday today. We do it every summer for the boss, our owner, Smiley Smith. Smiley is a Broadway producer. He has us do a real show instead of one of those amateur nights most teams have. We used to have guys on this team who couldn't sing Happy Birthday without making a mistake. We're doing *Man of La Mancha* this year. I'm the backup Don Quixote.

Shocker does a lot of yelling about taking the exhibitions seriously but nobody does. That's the other thing about Smiley Smith. He always plays at least one series of downs for us at free safety in the opening exhibition. Shocker made the mistake one year of telling him he could have been a terrific player. So our whole game plan revolved around keeping Smiley Smith from getting killed.

August 6

We played our first exhibition, against the Browns, and lost 24—20. We scored two touchdowns and two field goals, and Johnnycake and I were beautiful. I didn't play in the real game but I was in mid-season form on the sidelines. The most important part of being a second-string quarterback is to look helpful and involved. I love to wear the head phones up to the scouts in the press box. They're lunatics, yelling and screaming in the telephone so much that I can hardly hear the plays they're sending down. What I do is I make up the plays myself as we go along and pass them on to the staff. I've been doing it for three years and nobody knows it yet. The topper is that when I do get to play they always send the plays in for me. This is some madhouse. Incidentally, Smiley didn't get killed.

August 9

I have to tell you about Scotty Scott, our great all-pro tackle. He's the most admired man on this team. He's bald but he's got a commercial for a dandruff remover. He can't drive but he has an automobile commercial. And he plugs both of them in every interview. He's my idol.

August 13

We played the Bears tonight. Smiley took over a bunch of high school cheerleaders and led the cheers, for Christ sake. Six-Six played the last quarter and looked poised. I took him under my wing on the sideline and gave him the benefit of all my years of wisdom.

"Kid," I said, "the first one who talks in the huddle, listen to him. Keep listening until you find which guys are most reliable. And study your tarot cards."

We lost 24—20 again. I held for the two field goals and one extra point. Six-Six held for the other extra point. Johnnycake kicked it right through. I'm not worried. I shouldn't be worried. But why am I worried?

The madmen in the press box, our scouts, got into a scuffle with two fans outside their booth. Damned if Smiley didn't race up there and break it up.

August 18

Something's happening. Johnnycake and Six-Six practiced kicking all afternoon. I bumped into Johnnycake in the head late tonight and asked him what was doing.

"Shocker said to work with the kid," Johnny-cake said.

"I understand that," I said. "We've been through this before. But the kid's good. And you weren't missing."

"Cool it," Johnnycake said. "If he does well all week and I blow one in a game he'll start pressing."

August 20

I know why I was worried now.

The Patriots beat us 24—20 tonight, and Johnnycake didn't miss. Six-Six put the ball down and Johnnycake kicked it, simple as that. And I've been making a science out of it in the newspapers for years. You've got to put your hands here, the index finger here, the whole thing. Six-Six just puts the ball down.

I had to fight myself to keep from demanding an explanation from Johnnycake on the sideline. I was distracted: this time Smiley got into a scuffle and the scouts saved him. The fans were singing, "Good-by Shocker, Good-by Shocker, Good-by Shocker, we hate to see you go." Smiley got mad. He just gave Shocker a lifetime contract, and it's a little premature to tell him he's dead.

August 23

I got blind-sided today. When you're thirty-three that doesn't do you any good.

Johnnycake told me this morning he got a better deal with the kid.

"Three thou," he said. "And a two thousand dollar bonus if he replaces you as the backup QB. I'm sorry, it's a business deal. You understand."

I understood.

A second thing hit me at the afternoon practice. Shocker was going around prodding his linemen—they don't even yell ouch any more, I think they kind of like it, to tell the truth—when he told me I'm playing this week. Here goes nothing.

When it rains it pours.

August 27

There was no pie in the sky for old quarterbacks tonight. The Bengals beat us 24–20.

Six-Six started and had a typical up-and-down half for a rookie. But he threw the ball like he can throw the ball. As for me, you've heard of the look-out block, where the blockers yell "look out" as the guy they're supposed to block rushes at the quarterback. Well, I throw look-out passes. When I yell "look out" everyone looks out for an interception. I threw three look-outs in the second half.

The press box scouts weren't as much of a mess as usual. Smiley was up there with them and he did all the talking. The only position Smiley watches is the free safety, his position. Sonofagun, if he didn't come over pretty good. That's the first coherent phone conversation I've had with a scout in about eight years.

September 3

They cut the squad down to forty today. Guess what? I don't know how I look but I feel bloody. They gave me a job as an upstairs scout.

I knew I was gone when Shocker tapped me on the shoulder with his sword. But you have to love the guy.